Knowledge, Evolution, and Paradox

SUNY Series, the Margins of Literature
Mihai I. Spariosu, Editor

Knowledge, Evolution, and Paradox

The Ontology of Language

Koen DePryck

State University of New York Press

Original drawings (Figure 2, 13, 14, 15, 16, 17, 18, 19, and 20) by Koen DePryck and Dominique Vermeersch.
Figure 1. Paul Klee, *Landschaft mit dem Galgen* courtesy Schwabe & Co Verlag, Basel. From: Klee, P. *Das bildnerische Denken*, 5. Auflage, 1990, p. 77.
Photograph courtesy G. Clements, New York.

Published by
State University of New York Press, Albany

Printed in the United States of America

For information, address State University of New York Press, State University Plaza, Albany, N.Y., 12246

Production by E. Moore
Marketing by Theresa A. Swierzowski

Library of Congress Cataloging-in-Publication Data

DePryck, Koen, 1962-
Knowledge, evolution, and paradox : the ontology of language / Koen DePryck.
p. cm.—(SUNY series, the margins of literature)
Includes bibliographical references and index.
ISBN 0-7914-1533-3 (alk paper).—ISBN 0-7914-1534-1 (pbk. : alk paper)
1. Language and languages—Philosophy. I. Title. II. Series.
P106.D456 1993
401—dc20 92-26006
CIP

10 9 8 7 6 5 4 3 2 1

To Mark Van Steertegem,
a friend and mentor.

Contents

Illustrations

Acknowledgments

I am grateful to all the people with whom I have had the privilege of working during the past years, both in Ghent (Belgium) and Dallas, Texas. I want to mention particularly Alex Argyros, Karel Boullart, David Channell, Stephanie Grilli, Gretchen Sween, and Frederick Turner. Mark Van Steertegem was the first to direct me to the philosophical path that has eventually led me to this work. His unconditional confidence has meant more to me than I can ever express. To him I dedicate this work: Students can be grateful—sometimes. My wife, Dominique, and our daughters, Debra, Sharleena, and Ezra, have been the victims of my drive to understand the world—for which I apologize. During the time I spent in Dallas to work on this project, Hubert and Liesbeth Flamant became close friends. One does not often meet people like them. Aagje Van Cauwelaert did a terrific job reading the manuscript. She has made this a better book. Marleen Van Waeyenberge provided logistic support. A major part of the research in this book was made possible through the Belgian National Fund for Scientific Research.

Chapter 1

INTRODUCTION

Entwickeln wir, machen wir unter Anlegung eines topographischen Planes eine kleine Reise ins Land der besseren Erkenntnis.
Let us, by drawing a topographical map, make a small journey into the land of better knowledge.
—Paul Klee, Schöpferische Konfession

UNDERSTANDING AN EVOLVING WORLD

The challenge of this work is that of trying to understand the fundamental unity and diversity of everything—including ourselves—that exists and continues to emerge within an evolutionary framework. That framework is not intrinsically or exclusively biological in nature. Biology, as I will argue throughout this book, is part of a more general ontological framework that, by definition of ontology, embraces every single discipline and that is explicitly interdisciplinary in nature. Biology, of course, is the discipline par excellence where one can find well-defined and elaborated models of evolution, including a good amount of established and more or less commonly known terminology. Biological evolution could therefore be thought of as a metaphor describing the totality of the world in terms of a general structure of relations among parts of the world that are themselves studied by more specific disciplines. However interesting such a verbal exercise might be, it would nevertheless also keep some of the most fundamental aspects of interdisciplinarity out of our cognitive reach. Interdisciplinarity, I will argue, cannot be a reduction of our knowledge to a single discipline—either as a metaphorical extrapolation of a discipline, or as the quest for a single formula from which the totality of the world would emerge.

I understand that the study of an individual discipline can be very rewarding and stimulating. However, such an endeavor does restrict the scope of our perspective on reality. Of course, it is quite obvious that it is no longer possible for an individual to possess all the knowledge in the world. As a matter of fact, most disciplines can no longer be known in their entirety by a single scholar. It appears as if a reduction of all knowledge to a single formula or at least a very restricted set of basic principles is indeed our only hope to be truly interdisciplinary one day.

By the time I finished art school and started thinking about college, I found it very hard to find one discipline more interesting or more appealing than another. "An eclectic mind" was what a counselor called it. I never figured out whether he meant it as a compliment or not. Anyway, in the end I decided to enroll as a philosophy student at the University of Ghent, because they offered a program that allowed students to select at least a part of the course work from other disciplines taught at the university. As a result of that approach I was able to study a variety of seemingly very distinct subjects, including mathematics, biology, African literature, and aesthetics. What struck me most, however, was how similar all those subjects were, not in the sense that African and Western literature could be substituted for one another, but in the way two paintings—two landscapes, for example—can recall each other even though they are made by very different people in very different times. I guess that similarity was not what the professors were trying to get across to us, for most of them engaged in an introduction devised to illustrate how specific and different their field of study was. I tried to be a good and respectful student, but I could not help it: My thoughts kept wandering across the borders of the disciplines. As I got (a little bit) older and (a lot) less respectful, similarity and difference became my main point of attention. How? Why? When? These were the major questions that, while I could not readily answer them, gradually shaped my thinking about an interdisciplinary ontology—by which I mean an ontology focusing on the grounds for the division of the world into distinct, but nevertheless related, parts that are studied by specific disciplines.

It seems reasonable to think about ourselves—humanity—in terms of being such a distinct part of the world. As a matter of fact, it is even tempting to think about ourselves as belonging to a *privileged* segment of the world, which leaves us with some fundamental questions about the relation between ourselves and the totality of reality. But before we can consider possible answers, we must ask and answer the basic onto-epistemic question: How can a part understand the totality to which it belongs?

Crucial to an interdisciplinary ontology and how we can know about it—what we might call an "interdisciplinary onto-epistemology"—is the notion of self-reference. Self-reference is fascinating: Do we not regard our ability to think about ourselves as one of our most powerful and meaningful cognitive features? Are we not puzzled by the question whether our brain, probably the most complex piece of matter in existence, will one day be powerful enough to understand itself? Do we not consider computers to be inferior to us, because lacking the reflexivity of our own thoughts, they supposedly are not aware of what they are doing?

Decartes's dictum, *Je pense, donc je suis,* is a reflexive statement about our cognitive powers. Regardless of whether Descartes is right, his point of view reflects upon an important matter, because our ontology is only as good as it is epistemically accessible. In other words, an ontology, if it is to be of any cognitive significance, must guarantee that we can know something about it. That means that it must be possible, from an epistemological point of view, for the ontic level to refer to itself. An ontology must contain its own epistemic agent, its own spectator. In chapter 6 it will become clear how important that condition is, as it makes it possible to assume that the quantum-physical level of reality must in principle—ontically—be able to refer to itself and therefore contain its own observer, an observer so crucial to the specific interpretation of quantum physics.

Self-reference entails self-similarity. Even an extremely simplified version of chaos theory tells us that much. It makes good sense, too. A thought about a thought is still a thought. As a matter of fact, it would come somewhat as a surprise if thinking about thinking were to be completely different from thinking. Were we to find out that thinking, on the one hand, and thinking about thinking, on the other, are indeed two fundamentally different processes, we consequently would have to give up the reflexivity of our thinking. Our winning cognitive act would instantly lose much, if not all, of its glamour and collapse to a level comparable to talking about eating or dreaming about sex—nice to do when on a diet or alone, respectively, but definitely not as interesting as the real thing.

If self-reference entails self-similarity, does that mean then that reference implies similarity? Talking about a recipe for lasagna, for example, bears most certainly at least a structural resemblance to actually preparing the real thing. We can list the ingredients, add them in the right order, and put dinner in the oven for a specified amount of time without as much as moving a finger. A slight movement of the tongue and some other parts involved in producing sound will suffice. Mentally rehearsing the recipe, we could even get by with some neurochemical imbalances in our brain.

The question concerning reference and similarity is this: If our language and our knowledge refer to the world, does that mean that they are somehow "like" the world, that they structurally resemble the world? In the case of the recipe for lasagna, that claim is not so hard to defend. But what about a poem, an abstract painting, or a paradox? Can chemistry refer to physics?

I am, or at least so I am told, a fundamental optimist. I spend a great deal of time thinking about thinking, and I do like to think that those thoughts are not just a pleasant but unreal dream. On the other hand, however, some epistemic modesty might be called for. Why would I be so different from the rest of the world? By "rest of the world" I do not mean just "other people" but literally everything else in the world. Elaborating on that structural similarity, should I not admit that since I can reflect upon myself, the world too can reflect upon itself?

A traditional version of this thesis has it that the world is reflexive because we, as human beings, are reflexive. After all, we are a part of the world and not some innocent bystanders who just happened to be in the neighborhood. The argument grants us a monopoly on reflexivity but allows the whole world to participate in our glory.

I think we should do better and acknowledge that reflexivity—including epistemic self-reference—is an essential operation throughout reality and not just in our human cognitive realm. We have thoughts that reflect upon thoughts—that is one layer of reflexivity—but those other thoughts reflect upon the world outside our thoughts—that is another layer of reflexivity, a layer that is definitely not exclusively human. Granted, the two types of reflexivity are not identical, but that, I believe, is precisely the point: Reflexivity changes in nature as it continues to emerge as one of the most powerful cognitive features. Given this humble realism (only realists can be truly optimistic) we might start looking for reflexivity outside the human realm. We no longer need to assume that reflexivity and what it entails (for instance, paradoxes) belong exclusively to the language we use to describe the world. Our language, rather, is reflexive, but it belongs to a fundamentally reflexive world.

Grounds for an Interdisciplinary Ontology

If the world is indeed in essence a self-similar, chaotic structure, it becomes very hard to consider one level of reality to be more important than another, even when we consider a preceding level to be essential for the next level. Chemical reactions, for example, are a necessary condition for biological entities, but that does not mean that biology is more important than chemistry or vice versa. Every discipline, and not just biology, should therefore in principle be able to provide the necessary metaphors to describe at least partially the world beyond its own subject matter. In trying to give such partial descriptions, we discern an admittedly fuzzy image of an evolving evolution. That image, I believe, provides us with a key to understanding the dynamics behind the increasing differentiation of the world into domains or levels that are studied by specific disciplines. Evolving evolution and the structural differentiation generated in the process are therefore essential to an interdisciplinary ontology.

Is it too ambitious an undertaking to try to make such an ontology explicit? Maybe, and even probably, so, especially within the scope of a single book. Nevertheless, nobody should be misled into believing that disciplines belong to sanctioned experts—sanctioned by whom?—and that nobody but those experts has the right to talk about the relevance of any specific discipline for humanity. But then, of course, that is easy for me to say: I am not an expert.

I am, however, human—in the most literal sense of the word. Though it might sound trivial, it is nevertheless essential to point out that human beings are confronted with a number of questions, problems, and perspectives that are inherently linked to the boundaries within which the human race exists. These boundaries and the cognitive and other restrictions they imply relate to and must be specified for each of the different levels on which we exist: the indeterminate quantum world, the physiology of our body in general and especially the neurochemistry of our brain, the social and cultural environment in which we live, to name just a few. Some of the questions that are of the utmost importance for humanity—questions concerning guidelines for our behavior, questions concerning the validity and scope of our knowledge—relate to several, if not all, of those levels. They cannot and should not be answered by experts qua experts in a specific domain. These questions concern the grand scheme of the world; these questions concern how we fit into the big picture, not just on one single level but on all levels simultaneously.

To the extent that these are real questions, they deserve real, if perhaps necessarily incomplete, answers. Not just any answer will do. Answering these questions is not just a matter of individual conviction, as we are sometimes led to believe in the name of a naively understood "plurality," "democracy," or "freedom." Even when we accept that everybody is "entitled"—but by whom?—to his or her own personal beliefs and answers to these questions, that does not imply that all those answers are equally valid, not even if it were possible to prove that we cannot, in principle, know exactly which answers are true and which false.

A major purpose of this work is to investigate the grounds, if any, on which we can answer these fundamental questions, as well as the tools to do so. It turns out that such an investigation, in a reflexive movement in which the investigation turns to itself, answers the very questions it attempts to deal with: The grounds to answer the questions turn out to be the answer to the questions. Evolution, specifically, is a ground as well as an objective for our actions. Everything we do, think, or feel is necessarily subjected to the general rules of evolution. At the same time, we determine, select, or even adapt specific evolutionary rules to what is happening on a larger scale. Whenever we get the impression that we are breaking the rules and that we are outsmarting nature, we are actually just changing the rules of a game that has changing rules as its principle. Sometimes we win, sometimes we lose—and we do not decide on that. We can only play the evolutionary game and try to be creative at it: Evolution decides if we are or not.

That grounds for answers turn out to be the answers themselves does not mean that the answers are just begging their own questions, at least not in a way that would trivialize the project of interdisciplinarity. One could think about it as dealing with problems raised by language, in language. Although this reflexive movement will certainly impose certain limits on the scope and possible results of such a project, it does not mean that it should be abandoned altogether. I will argue, as a matter of fact, that precisely the restrictions related to self-reference allow us to proceed with these investigations in the first place.

Not only might one think about using language to deal with problems raised by language as similar to the reflexive nature of this interdisciplinary project; I believe that this is exactly what the reflexivity is about: reflexivity of language.

Obviously, the reflexivity of our human language can hardly be considered as a ground for what is going on at the level of physics, chemistry, or biology. However, at those levels, too, we might discover a fundamental reflexivity, accounting for the reflexivity of our own language, which has evolved out of the preceding levels, out of the preceding languages of the world.

In my attempt to formulate a minimal ontology based on the reflexivity of the world, I never felt as if I were stripping reality from its flesh, laying bare a bony structure too meager to be of any cognitive significance whatsoever. Crossing the borders between disciplines and languages, I discovered an incredibly rich but also incredibly simple framework in which variation and differentiation are provided and accounted for by the intrinsic nature of the evolutionary concepts and processes that are maintained as building blocks of reality.

I believe that the strength of this work lies in the unyielding way in which it takes processes and concepts such as language, evolution, and performance beyond the scope of humanity, beyond culture, even beyond biology, chemistry, and physics. It takes them to the world in all its aspects—as far as we can take them before being confronted with the unavoidable and intrinsic limits of our human perspective.

The Reflexivity of Languages

Reflexivity is essential to what we can do within the boundaries of our language. Not only do we refer to and reflect on other people's words when we use language, but we also reflect on our own words. This book was not written in a straight line leading from the first word on the first page to the last word on the last page. It was, rather, layered, as one would layer paints. Unavoidably it interferes with itself.

This text is not as much a review of existing research as it is the account of what Paul Klee calls "a journey into the land of better knowledge." It has been, and still is, a reflexive journey full of unexpected panoramic views, déjà-vu experiences, dead ends, circular movements. There is interference with other minds, with words spoken by other people, with images, odors, and sounds. The interference patterns caused by those encounters are recorded; the specifics, however, are often forgotten.

A fragment of a text by Paul Klee and a reproduction of one of his paintings illustrate strikingly how reflexivity operates as chaotic iteration. They do so as well on the level of each of them taken separately, on the level of their mutual interaction and interference, as on the level of how they were brought together.

Klee himself has published only a minor part of his work. After his death, Klee's wife handed over most of Klee's intellectual estate to Jürgen Spiller, at that time still an art history student. In 1956, Spiller published *Das Bildnerische Denken,* a collection of previously unpublished texts. While Spiller certainly reproduced all of them, he inserted paragraphs and drawings from other periods of Klee's work and teaching, going as far as adding some of his own drawings and interpretations without explicitly identifying them as such to his readers.[1] Although subsequent editions have been annotated to some extent, this somewhat unorthodox approach quite obviously jeopardizes the usefulness of Spiller's edition as a source for scholarly work. However, during my research at the Paul Klee Stiftung in Bern, Switzerland, it became clear to me that Spiller had done exactly what I believe that Klee himself would have appreciated most. Spiller had interacted with Klee's world and reported on that encounter. True, Klee's work deserves to be made available in its original form, but the only way to do so would be the publication of a facsimile edition of the three thousand or so pages with notes, sketches, and so forth. The manuscripts are so rich in their visual organization—layout, calligraphy, the use of color, etc.—that any alternative would be even more "untrue", and definitely less interesting, than Spiller's. The key here, I think, is that the nature of the specific questions Klee tries to answer invites such an interaction. Even stronger: Such an interaction is the only appropriate, authentic response to those questions.

Notes in Paul Klee's own copy of his *Schöpferische Konfession* indicate that he used this text (which he started to write in 1918 and first published in 1920 in *Tribune der Kunst und Zeit*) in his teaching at the Bauhaus. Of the five sections of the text, which in total is not longer than about four pages, I have translated the second, which describes—or, rather, undertakes—"a journey into the land of better knowledge." The text as it appears in Spiller's edition is an exact reprint from the original publication, although Spiller included two of Klee's paintings from that period to illustrate the essence of the text. Although strong connections can be found between the text and the paintings, the choice has been Spiller's and not Klee's. However, Spiller's choice is far from arbitrary. In the catalogue at the Paul Klee Stiftung in Bern, I have looked at reproductions of almost every single painting made by Klee in the period relevant to this text (1918–20). Klee meticulously kept records of his work, so the extent of his oeuvre is well defined, and Spiller's choice can be described as more than adequate. I include *Landschaft mit dem Galgen*, which relates to the section of the text translated here. (See figure 1.)

> Let us, by drawing a topographical map, make a small journey into the land of better knowledge. Beyond the still point, the first active movement takes place (line). After a while we rest, take a breath (interrupted line or, when we stop more than once, an articulated line). We look back to see how far we have come (opposite movement). We mentally dwell upon the way to that place and again to that place, which is now different

FIGURE 1.
Landschaft mit dem Galgen, Paul Klee. 1919/115. Oil on cardboard. Private collection, New York.

(a bundle of lines). A river will hinder, we take a boat (wavelike movement). Farther up there would have been a bridge (a series of arcs). On the other side we meet a kindred soul, also trying to get to the place where more knowledge is to be found. At first united in joy (convergence), we find ourselves more and more diverging (two lines following their own course). On both sides, a certain emotionality (expression, dynamic, and soul of the line).

We cross a ploughed field (a surface crossed with lines), then a dense wood. The other gets lost, hunts for the way, making the classic movement of a hound looking for a trace. But I am also losing my self-confidence; mist is hanging over another area, crossed by rivers (spatial element). Yet it will be soon clearing up again. The basket weavers are on their way home with their cart (the wheel). Traveling with them is a child with curly hair (spiral movement). Later the air gets sultry and nocturnal (spatial element). Lightning on the horizon (zigzag line). Above us still, some stars remain visible (a seed-bed). We soon reach our first quarters. Before we fall asleep, memories will cross our mind, as even such a small journey leaves us full of impressions.

A diversity of lines. Spots. Dots. Smooth surfaces. Rough-hewed, striped surfaces. Wavelike motion. Hampered, articulated movement. Opposite movement. Weaving, fabric. Brickwork, scales. Unison. Many voiced. Fading, thickening line (dynamism).

After the serene regularity of the first part: restraints, nerves! Restrained tremors, caresses of the soft wind. Insects get nervous before the thunderstorm. Anger, murder. The good cause as a guide-line, even in thicket and twilight. Lightning recalled that fever graph. Of a sick child . . . then.[2]

In this text, Klee takes us on a journey that, when read from the first sentence toward the last, is not linear in nature. The normal direction of causation has come apart. The first sentence and the last happen simultaneously, but also they do not: We cannot simply read the text twice as if we had not made the journey before. Neither can your eyes move over the canvas and reach the same spot twice without triggering some sort of remembrance. The text is not a translation of the painting, nor is the painting an illustration of the text.

Nevertheless, they exist in a close relationship to each other, in a complex and figurative, nonlinear relation that reflects the complexity and the nature of the very world they refer to and reflect upon.

For a long time, I implicitly assumed that most of the concepts that I was dealing with—entropy, chaos, order, evolution, and so forth—were essentially figurative, visual concepts that I used in my own paintings. I did not think of them as discursive verbal terms embedded in or constituting scientific theories. It is only later that I started to investigate the discursive verbal aspect of the concepts I had been using all along. Since those concepts also constitute the spine of this book, a figurative, visual perspective on reality is essential to the ideas developed in it.

However, figurative visual thinking cannot as such be present in this text, which is, rather, the record of the interference between a discursive verbal, a discursive visual, a figurative verbal, and a figurative visual thinking—similar in nature to Klee's verbal description of his both verbal and visual journey to the land of better knowledge.

To the extent that this text is verbal and discursive, I believe that some of the "leaps" in it cannot be resolved. They are, in fact, not really leaps. They are a pattern resulting from the interference of figurative simultaneity with the linearity of the argumentative structure of the text. Although it is something the reader should be aware of, I do not consider this to be a problem. On the contrary: I think this interference, while admittedly taking away from the discursiveness, allows me to talk about things that cannot be talked about in any other way.

Of course, the figurative aspects of my work should not be allowed to contradict a discursive understanding of the world. I will argue, as a matter of fact, that coherency is a fundamental onto-epistemic value. However, coherency does not and should not imply reduction: The coherency of figurative and discursive language does not imply that figurative language can be completely reduced to discursive language.

This work, then, rather than attempting to present a carefully balanced and systematic account of the relations and differences between verbal and nonverbal, and between discursive and figurative, language, uses those relations and differences to make a more general onto-epistemic point about our language in relation to the other languages of the world. As such, this work is as much a philosophical investigation of language as it is an attempt to establish a language of philosophy. That reflexive movement is crucial, I believe, to any authentic use of language. Reflexivity is a condition for evolution and therefore a condition for existence. But not only is it a ground for evolution, it is also an intrinsic goal: Reflexivity is an emerging feature of the universe.

This approach to interdisciplinarity imposes certain fundamental restrictions on what I can hope to accomplish—not only within the limited scope of this work but also as an onto-epistemic system in general. But I will present these restrictions as essential to the possibility of saying something meaningful in the first place. If I could say just anything whatsoever, or if I were able only to say what is true, what would be the point in saying something in the first place? In the first case, my language would be completely arbitrary. In the second case, it would be totally useless and probably nothing more than the expression of the extreme boredom of being an omniscient creature.

The Virtues of Realism

In this work I argue that a fundamental realism is a necessary condition for the nontriviality of our thinking—a point I will take as far as a claim for mathematical realism. While such a realism, in general, imposes restrictions on our cognitive abilities and our freedom, I believe that such restrictions are what make understanding and freedom possible in the first place. Such realism—in the sense of reference to the world and as opposed to an endless loop of references among signs on the same level, as some contemporary philosophers would like us to believe—is the only thing that can make our constraints meaningful.

Realism, however, should not be confined to discursive verbal statements. One of the important steps toward interdisciplinarity implies precisely that we start taking both verbal and nonverbal figurative language seriously, that we start granting nonverbal and figurative language the same cognitive status as discursive verbal language.

Artists live in the world of reality, a reality in which they have to orient themselves. Art does not, therefore, free humanity from reality, but rather is an important tool for comprehending reality. At the same time, however, art contributes to the world, to the development of our environment. The history of art, in Charles Biederman's terms, is a series of statements about reality. Progress in art can be accomplished by eliminating fantasy and replacing it with ever-greater correspondence to the actual world. This does not imply that an academic "realism" can or should be put forward as the final goal of art. "As with our comprehension of nature," Biederman defends his position, "art is a never ending process of new discoveries and new realization—a matter of development, growth—a natural growth."[3]

Not very often does one find such a strong and confident expression of not only the cognitive nature of visual language but also the evolutionary power of art. This is the evolutionary mentality that I hope will come across in this work: an approach that focuses on the crossroad between what is and what can be, an approach grounded in a fundamental history of previously fulfilled conditions that have led to the world as we know it and the new possibilities created thereby.

As far as my own work is concerned, I can only hope that it meets some of the conditions for further evolution of our human understanding that were previously unfulfilled. I have attempted to indicate some elements that I find important—interdisciplinarity, an explicit integration of verbal and nonverbal, and discursive and figurative, language, and so on—based on an analysis of the most general ontic processes and concepts—evolution, paradox, chaos, probability, interference, and others. The terminology that I have used to build that universal, but minimal, framework relies on a metaphoric extension of a more discipline-specific terminology that, by necessity, has to reflect the basic ontic structure as well as the more level-specific aspects. Also, while this work explicitly deals with the ontic and the onto-epistemic structure of the world, the epistemic question itself—How can we know those structures?—is addressed only implicitly, namely, in the simultaneous and thus necessarily figurative look at a multitude of disciplines and in the attempt to discern the pattern that links them all together. In that sense, this work is irreducibly artistic, in that it could not have been written without that attitude. That is the answer to the question I presented earlier: How can poetry or an abstract painting refer to the world? In its overall coherence, the world itself is artistic—a poem or an abstract painting bringing together the most diverse disciplines.

I recognize that this work inscribes itself in a growing intellectual and cultural tendency toward integration. It participates in the quest for unity in diversity and, as I will argue, diversity because of fundamental unity. Such a program, I believe, is more than just academic. It investigates on the grounds of the most essential conditions for our existence—as we can trace them throughout the history of evolution, not only of biological and cultural evolution, but of the evolution that started when time and space were first created—which options, if any, are open to us. Is that important? Should we even care? It is obvious that we can live our lives without even once bothering to ask, "Why?" I believe, however, that for the very first time we are in a position from which we can start to discern a possible answer or the conditions under which an answer to that troublesome question could be suggested, especially as we are finding out how to rephrase the question. That, ultimately, is what this work attempts to do: contribute to rephrasing the fundamental question that we cannot escape from—the question about ourselves.

Chapter 2

An Interdisciplinary Framework

The poet's eye, in a fine frenzy rolling,
Doth glance from heaven to earth, from earth to heaven;
And as imagination bodies forth
The forms of things unknown, the poet's pen
Turns them to shapes, and gives to aery nothing
A local habitation and a name.
—*Shakespeare,* A Midsummer Night's Dream

The Onto-Epistemic Horizon of Knowledge

The goal of this adventure, this journey into the land of better knowledge, is to put forward a minimal framework to contain and structure everything we know, or what we believe we know, about the world and ourselves. This project is therefore explicitly interdisciplinary in the sense that it attempts to embrace, validate, and/or reject our discipline-specific knowledge within a more general framework.

However, the success of the search for interdisciplinary coherence should not be taken for granted. As a matter of fact, neither should the quest itself. Although it appears that the climate is gradually changing, individual disciplines—perhaps I shoud rather say "individual scientists"—resist not only interdisciplinarity but also any specialized knowledge coming from outside their own more or less restricted and defined domain.

Werner Heisenberg, in *Physics and Beyond,* describes how he started his academic career as a student of mathematics. His father arranged for him to meet Ferdinand von Lindemann, a famous mathematician. Heisenberg recalls that during their meeting, Lindemann asked him what books he had recently been reading. Heisenberg mentioned Weyl's *Space, Time, and Matter.* While the professor's dog—who considered Heisenberg as an intruder in the domain of his master—kept up his yapping, Lindemann told Heisenberg that in that case he was completely lost to mathematics. That was the end of his interest.[1]

The rigid, protective structure of disciplines maintained in universities, libraries, and other highly valued places is more important than the anecdotic value of Heisenberg's amusing recollection may suggest. Such a rigid structure resists attempts toward changes and adds to the confusion between interdisciplinarity, by which I mean the study of the fundamental relations between sciences or disciplines, and multidisciplinarity—roughly either the use of techniques from one discipline within another or the study of a single subject by several disciplines.

Interdisciplinarity is not just a matter of improving methodology or stimulating the collaboration between disciplines. Working on the use of information systems in libraries, Stephen Bulick, a member of the technical staff at Bell Telephone Laboratories, investigates how a library comes to terms with knowledge and how "individuals come to terms with the library's terms reveal something about our understanding of knowledge."[2] He thereby assumes that the library behavior of scholars can be used to understand their overall knowledge-seeking behavior and more specifically how the subjects (defined as "Library of Congress Subclasses") consulted by the members of a given discipline ("academic departments") allow one to make assertions about the intellectual concerns of a discipline. Bulick's observations point at disciplinary diversification related to content and methodology, which leads to a confusion between multidisciplinarity and interdisciplinarity maintained in the structure of libraries and academic institutions. When two scholars belonging to two different academic departments collaborate on a project, they might get the impression that they are engaged in an interdisciplinary project, while they really are only operating at the fuzzy, multidisciplinary edges of their own disciplines.

It is necessary to establish a sound onto-epistemic foundation on which a true interdisciplinary theory can be built. Interdisciplinarity can exist only as interdisciplinary ontology, which in turn depends on the extent to which it is epistemically accessible to us.

The search for such an onto-epistemic foundation consists of the investigation of the necessary conditions that determine the existence and functioning of an interdisciplinary framework. The necessary conditions cannot but precede the interdisciplinary understanding: They determine its ontological and epistemological horizon. Ontologically they determine the extent to which the world is more than just a set of unrelated, completely independent facts—on the level of a single discipline as well as on the interdisciplinary level. Epistemologically the conditions determine to what extent we can understand the world. These ontological and epistemological questions cannot be dealt with independently from one another. Understanding the world, regardless of the extent of our knowledge, implies an understanding of its structures and relations. These structures and relations in turn determine to what extent they can access themselves and thus also to what extent they can reflect upon themselves. The necessary conditions therefore indicate the horizon of interdisciplinarity as being onto-epistemic: "Nothing" cannot be known, and "something" implies a minimal form of self-reference that can and should be qualified as knowledge. In the next chapters, I will return to that specific concept of knowledge and its consequences.

When we engage in a search for the onto-epistemic conditions of interdisciplinarity, some caution is called for. Because our understanding of the necessary conditions is itself subjected to those very conditions, we must trust that the self-reference involved in the process will not blind us completely. In other words, turning this upside down, we could ask ourselves under which onto-epistemic conditions we will not be completely blinded by the paradoxes that, as I will propose in the next chapter, are almost certain to occur in a complex self-referential system.

How many guarantees for success do we need? The history of philosophy as well as the history of science can be rewritten as attempts to attain absolute certainty. Ironically, the more certainty we try to attain, the more it becomes clear that uncertainty is the name of the game, that open-endedness is simply built into the system. What we are left with, basically, is the certainty of uncertainty. Once we understand that fundamental premise of our onto-epistemic position, we start to discern some answers. We will never have all the answers, but that does not mean that we cannot get any answers at all. However, if we reject the fundamental premise of our onto-epistemic position, we are at risk of not getting any answers at all.

As an investigation of the conditions of knowledge in general and interdisciplinary knowledge in particular, this work subscribes to the project of critical philosophy as it was explicitly established by Immanuel Kant. My use of "horizon" as an image to describe the problems facing interdisciplinary research explicitly acknowledges that relation and sets forth some of the implications of this work.

In the introduction to his *Logik,* Kant presents an outline of the problems critical philosophy is confronted with, the totality of which he indicates as its "horizon." Kant makes it very clear that knowledge needs to be established relative to the knowing subject: relative to any epistemic organism in general, but—as far as humans are concerned—especially relative to the human knowing subject. "When we expand or improve our knowledge," he wrote, "it is appropriate to consider the extent to which knowledge agrees with our goals and abilities. This reflection concerns the determination of the horizon of knowledge, which means the coherence between the totality of knowledge and the abilities and goals of the subject."[3]

The horizon of knowledge brings together world and subject, ontology and epistemology. This unity, as I understand it, solves the basic paradox of self-reference, namely, the seemingly impossible position of being both a subject and an object, of being both inside and outside one's environment. For Kant, the horizon of knowledge establishes the fundamental relation between ontology and epistemology in general, but the specific onto-epistemic perspective of interest to us is the human perspective created by the convergence of humankind and world at the vanishing point. Our cognitive horizon is a human horizon, in regard to its potential (limited by our epistemic powers) as well as in regard to its aims and goals (which have to be human). Since in principle we are not unlimited, since in particular we do not have the unlimited epistemic capabilities that would allow us to be completely disinterested in what exactly the knowledge is that we seek, we cannot but try to pursue knowledge that is in accordance with our limits and our finite existence. This may appear as self-evident and unavoidable, yet these limits have been blatantly disregarded by most traditional ontologies—ontologies that, implicitly or explicitly, put humanity in a position in which absolute knowledge becomes a given, as if we were able to put ourselves in a position outside the totality of the world without being also a part of that totality.

The horizon of knowledge concerns, in Kant's words, "die Beurteilung und Bestimmung dessen, was der Mensch wissen kann, was er wissen darf, und was er wissen soll": the investigation and determination of what we *can* know, what we *may* know, and what we *should* know.[4] The horizon of our knowledge, therefore, cannot but at the same time be political, ethical, aesthetic. Any theory of knowledge that tries to exclude these dimensions necessarily fails. Even stronger: Any such theory will necessarily be false. Knowledge, because of its existence at the intersection of subject and object, can never be completely "neutral." Neither can not-knowing ever be neutral. The post-Holocaust "We never knew," to mention just one striking example, cannot—ever—be an excuse: The Germans *should* have known and *could* have known. Although in fact some Germans may indeed not have known what was going on, this strengthens the point that knowledge—as well as not-knowing—is not only factually but also normatively partial.

Investigating the conditions of interdisciplinarity within that context will involve questions about the nature, the validity (with respect to our condition as human onto-epistemic organisms), and the possibility of the interdisciplinary project. These questions are essential, I believe, as they—in a reflexive movement—become questions about the nature, validity, and possibility of any knowledge, not just of interdisciplinarity. And in that same reflexive movement, these questions can be seen as the questions concerning essence.

Kant indicates the unity of knowledge as a condition imposed on the nature of knowledge. To grasp that unity, he introduces Self, World, and God as, respectively, a subject that can no longer be a predicate, a cause that cannot be an effect, and a totality that cannot be a part. These concepts express our attempts to reach an absolutely unified knowledge. Given our human finiteness, we need Self, World, and God, according to Kant, to pose the unity of knowledge. For Kant, however, these transcendental ideas are not to be seen as constitutive elements of our knowledge. They are regulative elements used to guide our experience, used to guide the thinking process. Self, World, and God are transcendental hypotheses that unify our external experience *as if* a "World" imposed it upon us. They unify our internal experience *as if* it were imposed by a transcendental "I," and they unify internal and internal experience *as if* they were both determined by an absolutely superior being: that is, "God."

The regulative unity, described by Kant, provides us with a unifying perspective on the world. The transcendental ideas determine the—imaginary!—vanishing point at the onto-epistemic horizon, and therefore they determine that horizon itself. The transcendental ideas have, in Kant's own words, "an excellent and indispensably necessary, regulative employment, namely, that of guiding the understanding toward a certain goal where all the strategies of its rules converge in one point from which, although a mere idea (*focus imaginarius*), the concepts of understanding do not really originate, since it lies completely outside the limits of possible experience; nonetheless it serves to give to the understanding the greatest unity as well as the greatest extension."[5] The regulative unity, according to Kant, is an imagined unity—not a unity at the level of the phenomena themselves—that should guarantee the unity and consistency of knowledge and therefore also of the actions taken based on that knowledge.

Kant's unifying concepts imply synthesis and integration. Knowledge, on the other hand, implies analysis and differentiation. What we need, then, in order to redefine Kant's answer in terms of constitutive rather than just regulative elements of our knowledge, without being at risk of engaging in illegitimate metaphysics, is a perspective, a horizon against which we can take things apart and bring them back together again. In doing so, we become both knowledgeable and wise.[6]

The horizon, I contend, is real: It is an essential element of our existence in the world and therefore of the world itself. I believe interdisciplinarity (and thus the unity it presupposes) is a phenomenon, in every sense of that word, that belongs as much to the world as to our understanding of the world. Interdisciplinarity offers an onto-epistemic perspective defining a human horizon, defining a horizon that shapes both the necessary conditions of the world or universe and the necessary conditions of humanity.

A Minimal Framework

In a specific way, this interdisciplinary study has interdisciplinarity as its subject. Any interdisciplinary framework should be, and cannot but be, minimal: It should contain the necessary conditions for coherence and nothing more. Attempts to obtain "maximal" interdisciplinarity have led to an abundance of types of interdisciplinarity on which people will never be able to agree, simply because they are much too focused on a specific perspective, rather than dealing with perspective as such.

Because maximal interdisciplinarity is mainstream, it is hard to find a consensus on what an interdisciplinary methodology requires and implies. One might even go as far as to say that interdisciplinarity is not yet defined as an autonomous field of research with its own subject. Gretchen Sween, in her article "Interdisciplinary Disorientation," comes up with no less than fourteen different approaches to interdisciplinarity—all of them currently being employed within one department at a single university! This diversity by itself she describes as "a challenge of identification."[7]

I believe that one of the reasons why interdisciplinarity has not yet been able to develop into a discipline in its own right is the confusion between interdisciplinarity and multidisciplinarity. It is obvious that the definitions of these terms—Which is which?—are ultimately arbitrary. Furthermore, it is equally obvious that inter- and multidisciplinarity cannot be totally autonomous, since interdisciplinarity must ultimately also account for the feasibility of a multidisciplinary approach. This by itself contributes to the problem at hand: making as clear as possible a distinction between inter- and multidisciplinarity.

In the social sciences (psychology, sociology, history, etc.) the use of both terms *interdisciplinarity* and *multidisciplinarity* to qualify one's research seems to indicate that inter-/multidisciplinarity assumes two basic forms: the study of subjects belonging to another field from the perspective of one's own discipline, and the use of methodology and tools originally developed in other disciplines to study subjects in one's own discipline. Science, for example, is studied as the social interaction among scientists. Economic models are used to describe social interactions in ancient societies. Demographic statistics are used to understand sociological patterns. Many other examples could be mentioned in an attempt to make a meaningful distinction between interdisciplinarity and multidisciplinarity. In doing so, we find that the terms are used interchangeably: The specific terminology used by different scholars boils down to a matter of taste.

I argue, however, that none of these examples involves interdisciplinarity in the sense that I will develop in this work. Before focusing on that "other" meaning, let us for a moment not make a distinction at all between inter- and multidisciplinarity and take a look at some of the established, although confusing, uses of the terminology.

History as a discipline has a special status among the social sciences. As a matter of fact, it is not even clear whether history should be labeled a "social science" at all. History as a discipline cannot easily be described in terms of its subject or its methodology; it seems to cross the traditional boundaries of disciplines, moving almost effortlessly between disciplines and their specific perspectives on the past. Sometimes this may lead to confusing situations, as in the case of the historian Frederick Jackson Turner who thought he was describing the *archaeology* of American life, while he was actually describing its *physiology.*[8]

As a result of this complex relation with perspectives and methods culled from a wide range of disciplines, history should at least in principle be more open to inter-/multidisciplinary research than any of the specific disciplines it embraces. And indeed, when Theodore Rabb and Robert Rotberg founded *The Journal of Interdisciplinary History* in 1970, they credited interdisciplinary "cross-fertilization" for an enriched understanding of the past. The new approach they advocated raised questions that were previously unasked, and research that once was thought impossible emerged from the new developments. When one closely reads their editorial of the first issue of the journal, it becomes clear that they see interdisciplinarity as a *technique,* or rather as the application in history of techniques that originated in other disciplines. "The questions previously unasked" turn out to be questions that could not be answered before because the *tools* to do so were not available. Consequently, Rabb and Rotberg solicited contributions focusing on the use of chemical analysis, economic models, statistics, genetic research, and so forth.

Somewhat arbitrarily, I call Rabb and Rotberg's project "multidisciplinary," whereas I call "interdisciplinary" the research that has as it subject, the relationship between, for example, mathematics and history—an internal relationship described in onto-epistemic terms.

The major point I want to make is that multidisciplinary pursuits leave the fundamental questions concerning the relations between disciplines unaddressed—in terms of both their subjects and their methods. Interdisciplinary studies are, namely, those studies that have as their subjects precisely these relations and their reference to the world.

One might argue that multidisciplinary research can lead to interdisciplinary research—that, for example, the use of statistics to do historical research might lead to a better understanding of the relation between probability and historical events. However, it should also be clear that interdisciplinarity is not a necessary consequence of multidisciplinarity. In 1982, Rabb and Rotberg published *The New History.* The book contains the results of a series of questions they presented to a diverse collection of leading scholars gathered at the Villa Serbelloni in Bellagio, Italy, in 1980—exactly ten years after they founded *The Journal of Interdisciplinary History.* The questions raised there, however, were still fundamentally the same as those raised in the first editorial of the journal. The shift from multidisciplinarity toward interdisciplinarity had not taken place.

On a pragmatic level, we could even argue that multidisciplinarity apparently resists the development of true interdisciplinarity. The assimilation of new ideas and techniques appears to disrupt the comfortable unity of the individual disciplines. It is obvious that the intellectual uncertainty that unavoidably accompanies this intellectual turmoil is far from ideal for starting to think about the fundamental unity and differentiation of the disciplines, especially because the intellectual animation originates from a methodological, and not from a semantic, concern. Synthesis becomes more and more difficult, patterns become harder and harder to recognize. At first the new techniques seem to widen the scope of traditional disciplines, but they ultimately lead to further differentiation and to further isolation within the field. Multidisciplinarity promotes a pluralism of approaches that renders synthesis even more difficult than it already is. Disciplines get caught in the dichotomy between functioning within a multidisciplinary context, on the one hand, and being part of a larger interdisciplinary project, on the other. This tension inspires the quest for maximal, rather than minimal, interdisciplinarity, a quest that makes interdisciplinarity tend toward multidisciplinarity in its desire to establish a single, unified science.

Not a Single Science . . .

There are reasons why interdisciplinarity has not yet developed into a mature discipline other than the fuzziness of the distinction between interdisciplinarity and multidisciplinarity, the resistance of individual disciplines to specialized knowledge coming from outside the discipline, or the structure of libraries and research institutes. While these reasons are essentially related to events taking place outside interdisciplinary research, it is necessary to consider some elements that are much more related to perspectives on interdisciplinarity itself.

Often it is simply assumed that interdisciplinary research will lead to a unified theory that will replace each of the individual disciplines. Especially to nonscientists, this seems a plausible project, particularly with respect to the so-called hard sciences: It seems intuitively reasonable to assume that, for instance, physics and chemistry have a common foundation that might one day replace the individual disciplines. The high degree of formalism realized by the hard sciences definitely contributes to that intuition. It appears that they already share a common ground in their common mathematical and symbolical formalism. For the so-called soft sciences or social sciences, however, such a replacement or reduction seems less likely. Here we do not find the highly formalized theories that constitute the hard sciences. Psychology, history, sociology, economics, and other disciplines appear fundamentally different. The same holds for the distinction between soft and hard sciences itself. Nevertheless, the search for a single, general discipline does not stop at these seemingly crucial distinctions.

Cognitive science—to elaborate somewhat on a specific example—is not a single discipline. Cognitive scientists are drawn from a whole range of disciplines—in particular, philosophy, psychology, artificial intelligence, linguistics, anthropology, and neuroscience. In other words, cognitive science crosses the border between individual hard sciences and individual soft sciences, and also the border between hard and soft sciences. Howard Gardner's *The Mind's New Science* is an attempt to summarize the accomplishments of cognitive science, which he defines as a new approach to epistemology, as "a contemporary, empirically based effort to answer long-standing epistemological questions—particularly those concerned with the nature of knowledge, its components, its sources, its development and its deployment."[9] Gardner puts interdisciplinarity forward as one of the basic features of cognitive science. He hopes that eventually the individual disciplines may blend together and yield a single, unified cognitive science. Although he does not claim that this approach might or should lead to a single, unified science in general—one not limited to epistemological questions, which he indicates as the subject of cognitive science—his claim is nevertheless an expression of the more general tendency of claims that the ultimate goal of science is to end up with just one discipline. That assumption, by the way, might very well account for at least part of the sometimes strong resistance against interdisciplinarity from specialists in any one field or discipline.

A minimal interdisciplinary theory should give maximal autonomy to each of the disciplines it embraces. There is no point in claiming that any theory has reached its limits. Every attempt to make such a claim has consistently been proven wrong, and there is no good reason to assume that the situation is now different. A clear example of an overly optimistic attitude with regard to the power of reductionism can be found, for instance, in Helmholtz's comment on the attempt of science to describe all natural phenomena in terms of simple forces between unalterable objects, an endeavor, conscious or unconscious, apparent in nearly all scientific thought throughout the two centuries following Galileo's time. "Finally, therefore," Helmholtz claims, "we discover the problem of physical material science to be to refer natural phenomena back to unchangeable attractive and repulsive forces whose intensity depends wholly on distance. The solubility of this problem is the condition of the complete comprehension of nature. . . . And its [science's] vocation will be ended as soon as the reduction of natural phenomena to simple forces is complete and the proof given that this is the only reduction of which the phenomena are capable."[10] For Helmholtz it was just a matter of details; but we can now reasonably assume that we have a long way to go before our understanding of physics will be complete—if, as we start to realize now, it can ever be complete at all! We should not make the same mistake as Nobel Prize winner Max Born, who in 1928 declared that physics would be over in six months from then. The conclusion is obvious: Each discipline should be provided with enough space to grow and change.

But a more general and fundamental point should be made. I believe that an interdisciplinary theory should not be proposed with the purpose of replacing each of the individual disciplines. Although the quest for the ultimate formula from which all the others would follow with necessity is an ancient one, it is my contention that each of the disciplines is unique and cannot be replaced by a general theory. That is not to say, of course, that the present distinction between disciplines such as physics, chemistry, and biology is accurate and should not be tampered with. As a matter of fact, the delimitation of disciplines might be one of the points where an interdisciplinary theory could interfere on the level of individual disciplines. Interdisciplinary theory is not just another metatheory, independent from, or without consequences for, each of the individual disciplines. Interdisciplinary theory will have a major impact on the coherence of individual disciplines and therefore on their existence as individual disciplines. In other words, interdisciplinary theory will contribute to the validation of individual disciplines.

As "philosophical speculation" and "natural philosophy" were replaced by, or changed into, "natural science" and "science," the claim has been made that philosophy should concern itself only with those questions that have as yet not been answered by science. As such, this does not imply a reduction of all knowledge to a single, general theory, but it does imply a reduction of all knowledge to a single scientific methodology, assumed to exist. From that position it seems to be but a minor step to a claim for a single, unified theory.

The strongest version of such a claim was made by logical positivism, attempting to establish a single unified science based on an axiomatic hypothetico-deductive logic à la Russell. The pamphlet *Wissenschaftliche Weltauffassung: Der Wiener Kreis*, published in the late 1920s by Carnap, Hahn, and Neurath, was intended to present a "philosophy to end all philosophies." In the authors' opinion, philosophy should limit itself not just to questions that had not yet been answered by science, but also to scientific concepts that, temporarily, needed further clarification that science could not yet provide. The basic assumption of this line of thinking—which sharply distinguishes between scientific and nonscientific, between experimental and nonexperimental—is obviously that given enough time all knowledge will be scientific and that philosophy therefore has almost outlived its usefulness.

Gradually, however, philosophy was brought back into the picture—although it is more accurate to say that philosophy tried very hard to reclaim its lost status—to function as some sort of supervisor, keeping track of the different specialties that very often had difficulty communicating with one another. Its new role, however, had become a pragmatic one, more related to the problems created by multidisciplinarity and the rigid structure of disciplinarity, as discussed earlier in this chapter, than to a move toward interdisciplinarity.

Obviously, the ever-increasing number of disciplines and subdisciplines made, and still makes, communication among scientists increasingly difficult. The fine structure of mathematical science, for example, consists of about three thousand categories or specialties, with most mathematicians rarely being in command of recent work in more than two or three areas. A fine mathematical collection such as the mathematics collection in The Brown University library consists of the equivalent of sixty thousand average-size volumes, a number that grows to about a hundred thousand if one includes material from related disciplines such as engineering and astronomy. More than sixteen hundred individual technical journals accept mathematical material, and nearly two hundred thousand theorems are published every year.[11]

If it has become almost impossible to keep up with even the more outstanding results in one's own field, how could one hope to keep track of what is going on in other fields? Overlooking the mass of highly specific research, philosophy was supposed to keep an eye on the big picture and offer a neutral zone where specialists could meet. Nevertheless, philosophy and philosophers were generally not prepared for that role. There was no tradition, there were no tools, there was not even a consensus on the subject.

Stephen Hawking, in *A Brief History of Time,* acknowledges that even if science were able to come up with a unified theory—which for him takes the form of a general theory in which all the other, partial theories are included as approximations—this would still be just a set of rules and equations, leaving the question *Why?* unanswered. Scientist have been too involved asking *What?*, and philosophers, "whose business it is to ask *why,*" cannot keep up with the rapid advance of scientific theories. Hawking sees answering this *Why?*-question as the most challenging task for philosophers and scientists alike. In other words, according to Hawking the quest for a unified theory does not in principle lead to a complete interdisciplinary theory that would also have to include the answers to the *Why?*-question. A unified theory, if one is at all possible, can only establish the relations among disciplines; it cannot explain them, it cannot breathe "fire into the equations."[12] This is a strong argument, especially coming from Hawking, who is thoroughly convinced of the value of the unified-theory project, for it would allow us to look into the mind of God, and whose work is a fundamental contribution to such a project.

My preliminary conclusion at this point is that even if a single unified theory were to be formulated, this theory would not be the ultimate interdisciplinary theory. Such a theory, of course, could provide a sound basis for interdisciplinary work yet to be done. The major problem left to consider for such a theory would be precisely what it attempts to do away with, namely, the differentiation between disciplines. Regardless of whether the actual boundaries between disciples are correct or not, the world itself appears to be differentiated into more or less autonomous subsets or substructures. The organization of knowledge in distinct disciplines has, in that sense, ultimately to do with the structure of the world itself. A unified theory should therefore never be reductionist; it should not be a search for a single formula that contains or entails all the others. Only when the increased differentiation could be seen as a single solution, or as a unique path toward such a solution, could a derivative of a single formula—this time describing that path—be argued for. In that case, however, our world would be completely determined, and I fail to recognize how in such a world there could ever be a need for differentiation, which, as I understand it, is an essential component of a system based on alternative solutions or alternative paths to solutions.

. . . And Not Deconstruction

That a single unified theory cannot be the prototypical interdisciplinary theory is only part of an answer to the question about conditions for interdisciplinarity. Maximal interdisciplinarity—for that is what the search for a reductionist unified theory really is—is ultimately a purely epistemic construction without an ontic foundation. As such, it is surprisingly closely related to the other end of the realm of possible approaches.

In the phenomenological tradition, a program, or rather a variety of still-changing programs, for philosophy is put forward. Based on the investigation of phenomena, this is to provide a new foundation for philosophy and science alike. In the value it attributes to experience, phenomenology is related to positivism, although it allows, besides the strictly sensory data to which positivists restrict themselves, such experiences as intuition to be taken into account. The term *intuition*, after all, stems from the Latin *intueri* which means "to perceive." According to Heidegger, one of phenomenology's major exponents, experience is something that "befalls us, strikes us, comes over us, overwhelms and transforms us"; it is something we undergo, that we endure, suffer, and receive as it strikes us, and that we submit to.[13] But phenomenologists contend that there is more to phenomena than is revealed in experience or, for that matter, in the semantic gradations of the language we use to discuss and to analyze them. Both experience and language—language itself being a form of experience—should therefore be used cautiously. Nevertheless, the study of phenomena makes it possible for us to obtain some fundamental understanding of the world in relation to ourselves.

The reasons to take a somewhat closer look at the relation between interdisciplinarity and phenomenology are manifold but can be more or less summarized in reference to one book: Jacques Derrida's *Edmund Husserl's The Origin of Geometry: An Introduction.*[14] As this is Derrida's first major published essay,[15] it is an introduction not only to Husserl's work and phenomenology in general but also to Derrida's own work.

Because Derridean deconstruction—together with postmodernism, its aesthetic counterpart—is so predominantly present in contemporary thinking, I believe that it is worthwhile to trace its background and to investigate some of its major ramifications for interdisciplinarity. Derrida is important to my work, because much of what is developed in the next chapters explicitly challenges his dismissal of logocentrism as "the 'myth' according to which language is guided by, subservient to, and can somehow mirror and latch on to, the true nature of nonlinguistic entities."[16]

Derrida's writing an introduction to Husserl does not mean that Derrida is a phenomenologist. It does mean, however, that he will formulate the questions he is dealing with within or against a phenomenological framework. Ultimately, he rejects that framework: In a later work, *Speech and Phenomena,* subtitled *Introduction to the Problem of Signs in Husserl's Phenomenology,* he concludes that "there never was any 'perception' " and that, ultimately, "contrary to what phenomenology—which is always phenomenology of perception—has tried to make us believe, contrary to what our desire cannot fail to be tempted into believing, *the thing itself always escapes.*"[17] Derrida, in other words, ends up denying the adequacy of experience in absolute terms. Neither experience in the positivist sense, nor experience in the extended, phenomenological sense, nor language as experience can give us access to the world. Neither philosophy (philosophical experience/language) nor science (scientific experience/language) can put an end to the reference from sign to sign. Their claims to refer to extralinguistic entities are metaphysical, "the metaphysics of presence" as Derrida calls it. Both science and philosophy can be only a form of writing, a system of signs in which signs get, or "create," meaning only in their relation to other signs that are part of the system. Derrida does not deny the existence of the world: He merely subsumes it under the heading of "text." The world becomes an integral and indistinguishable element of a text and can in no way be constructed as a condition for the existence of text. The distinction between "text" and "world" then becomes either trivial—as a distinction between two words with an identical meaning (although it is not clear how we could talk about "meaning" here)—or nonsensical, but never meaningful.

In his *Logical Investigations,* Edmund Husserl—probably the only common denominator to be found in the variety of phenomenological programs—attempted to show the flaws of the claim made by scientific psychology, or psychologism, that all knowledge is ultimately psychological in nature. Husserl pointed out that psychology, in order to be scientific (which, according to him, means that it has essence rather than fact as its object) needed to be incorporated in a larger structure that had to provide the minimal postulates on which a psychological science could be established. According to Husserl, this quest is related to the history of science and therefore ultimately to the history of knowledge. As Derrida points out in his comments on Husserl, it is even related to the awakening of a sense of history in general, where its phenomenological sense will merge with its teleological sense.[18] As follows from Husserl's definition of science as involved with essences (whatever those may be) rather than facts, the history of knowledge cannot be a history of facts: This would only lead us to historicism and its implied relativism. The history of knowledge has to be a history of essences. For Husserl, the ontic meaning of science—any science, but particularly geometry—"must have an origin in an accomplishment: first as a project and then in successful execution."[19]

History, however, cannot be just the development of a purpose already fully established from the beginning, in the origin. In that case, history would be reduced to the explanation of that beginning, of that origin, of that creation. It is therefore necessary to take "into account the fact that scientific thinking attains new results on the basis of those already attained, that the new ones serve as the foundations for still others, etc.—in the unity of a propagative process of transferred meaning."[20]

Logic, tied to language as well as to the ideal cognitive structures that arise specifically within it, can be described as "explication" (*Verdeutlichung*), as the making explicit of this unfolding history without actually reactivating the whole chain of premises. Doing this is the purpose of philosophy, so that, as Derrida rightly points out, Husserl's first important work, *The Philosophy of Arithmetic,* could have been entitled *The Origins of Arithmetic,* because despite its psychological inflection it is already concerned with "the reactivation of the primordial sense of arithmetic's ideal unities by returning to the structure of perception and the acts of a concrete subjectivity."[21] In *Formal and Transcendental Logic,* Husserl describes this project as an investigation into the subject of interdisciplinarity. Therefore, I believe, it is itself an interdisciplinary project, a project concerned with the essence of knowledge and the relation between the different epistemic disciplines, the "sciences." "These investigations," Husserl writes, "concerning the possible sense and possible method of genuine science as such, are naturally directed first of all to what is essentially common to all possible sciences. They should be followed secondarily by corresponding sense-investigations for particular groups of sciences and single sciences."[22]

Within his phenomenological framework, Husserl has established the need for a program for philosophy and science that is essentially interdisciplinary in nature. But he has done more than just that: He has outlined some of the conditions for such a project by indicating the horizon of the interdisciplinary project as being historical. Although we may know very little about that horizon, it has a definite structure that can be investigated, all the way back "to the primal materials of the first formation of meaning, the primal premises, so to speak, which lie in the prescientific cultural world." "Of course," he adds, "this cultural world has in turn its own questions of origin, which at first remain unasked." This remark puts Husserl's work in perspective. The history of knowledge is part of a larger historical project, one that embraces the "total problem of the universal historicity" of humanity and the cultural world. And then: "Still, questions like that of the clarification of the origin of geometry have a closed character, such that one need not inquire beyond those prescientific materials."[23]

It is at this point that my interdisciplinary project parts from Husserl's, although I trust I will remain faithful, in some sense, to his idea of historical reactivation. I believe the question concerning geometry cannot be solved without investigating its historical roots beyond the "prescientific material." Such a history (or evolution, as I would rather call it) is exactly what provides us with the anchors for our language—anchors that, as I will argue in the next chapter, link our human languages to the languages of the world. Derrida does not seem to find those links, because he extrapolates the phenomenologist claim that language does not suffice to access the world, to the point where language apparently no longer connects to the world at all. *Pars pro toto* is what we usually label that mistake: mistaking a part for the whole. It is neither because a part of our language unquestionably does not refer to a world outside itself, nor because some parts of the world cannot be accessed by our language, that we are entitled to conclude that "language" and "world" are two completely separate things without any meaningful connection. It is therefore clear that deconstruction cannot—ever—provide a basis for interdisciplinarity: From deconstruction's point of view, it is not even possible to make a clear distinction between disciplines. At best, disciplines appear as subtexts of a larger text, and neither text nor subtext has, as far as human beings are concerned, anything whatsoever to do with the world. This means that even if they did reflect some of the properties of the world, we would not be able to know about it. As a matter of fact, there would not be much left to know—not even whether deconstruction is right or wrong in its most fundamental claims.

Interdisciplinary Knowledge

Any attempt at interdisciplinarity will need to address the issue of language. At first sight, the problem is overwhelming. If two physicists, specialized in different fields, cannot communicate about anything but the most basic concepts of physics, how can we ever hope to be truly interdisciplinary? How can we ever hope to master each of the discipline-specific languages involved? Not being a physicist, it *is* frustrating trying to read Heisenberg's *The Physical Principles of the Quantum Theory,* although he himself claims in his preface (and I am sure he means it) that he has "been at pains to use only elementary formulas and calculation," adding "so far as that is possible."[24]

In light of the remarks presented in the previous chapter, it is rather obvious that interdisciplinary work cannot be reduced to a one-to-one translation of the terminologies used by the different disciplines. If such a translation were at all possible, it would follow that biology = chemistry = physics = culture, and so on. That would leave us with the question why, then, we make a distinction between the disciplines in the first place.

An obvious answer to that legitimate question would be that disciplines are just a matter of sociologically determined power structures. But Bulick's investigation of the use of library materials by scientists belonging to specific disciplines or specific departments of a university suggests that even though power structures and tradition (libraries, the departmental organization of universities, etc.) do play a role in keeping the existing structures intact, some consistency can be found in the delimitation of the subject matter that disciplines deal with.[25] Although that does not allow us to draw conclusions about the specific nature of the relationships among the different disciplines, this obviously does indicate that the disciplines deal with different territories.

One might think, of course, that disciplines are just a matter of different perspectives on the same thing, that disciplines share a common territory, only observed from different directions, from different angles. But that would only shift the question toward a question about the *why* of the different perspectives. Such a shift, as a matter of fact, would cut off our epistemology from the world. Different perspectives are meaningful only when they are tied to different aspects of that upon which one focuses and its relation to the environment. Our human perspective—including our visual perspective, which is both a part of and a metaphor for our cognitive perspective, just as language is both a part of and a metaphor for "the world of language"—is, of course, limited. We cannot see the back of a house when we stand in front of it. If we want to see the back of the house, we have to walk around it. In doing so, our perspective will shift, and we will end up with a more or less complete image of what the house looks like from the outside. My point now is that this is meaningful only because we live in a three-dimensional world, in a world where a house has a front and a back, a front and a back that are not identical. There is something we can learn from the shifting perspectives, something we would not be able to know without those shifts, which are therefore a necessary condition for more complete knowledge. The same holds for the inside-outside perspectives, and also—and here we come close to the question concerning the language of interdisciplinarity—for the perspectives of the physical and molecular structures of the house, its social function, its architectural value, and so forth. Therefore the language of interdisciplinarity cannot be the language of any of the individual disciplines: not of the most fundamental, nor of the most contingent.

Russell and Whitehead's classical but tragic attempt to integrate all possible knowledge was based precisely on the assumption that a reductionist approach, in the style of a "single unified theory," was feasible. Their project in *Principia Mathematica* can be described in two steps: first, the generation of all mathematics from a limited number of axioms, and second, the generation of all our knowledge based on mathematics. Gödel's incompleteness theorem—proving (on the basis of principles acceptable to Russell and Whitehead) that such a closed system of knowledge is in principle impossible—seemingly put a stop to that project.

I will argue, however, that Gödel's theorem—or rather that for which the theorem stands—is a necessary condition for an adapted, open-ended version of Russell and Whitehead's project to survive. In their version, it is hard to understand *why* we have nonmathematical knowledge (that is, knowledge not in the form of mathematics) in the first place. If all knowledge can be reduced to a logico-mathematical structure, why then do we have verbal language, poetry, art, and the like? Why do we not talk exclusively in terms of mathematical objects and logical operators?

It is one thing to claim that a logico-mathematical structure is *relevant* to art—which I believe it is indeed—but another to claim that art (or any other nonmathematical form of knowledge) can be *reduced* to such a structure. In the next chapters, I will introduce a structure, based precisely on the restrictions imposed by Gödel's theorem, that is generative in the sense that structures are generated from other structures but cannot be reduced to their origins. The language of interdisciplinarity, then, is the language of that process, which I claim to be essentially evolutionary in nature. In chapter 5, I will elaborate on the implications of that hypothesis.

It seems so tempting: If only we could replace all the individual disciplines by one convenient set of formulas, by one single language understood and spoken by all—we could be gods again. No longer would we be hindered by our myopic perspective on the world. We would have instant access to the whole realm of reality.

We are not gods. Another pertinent question then: Why are we not? Is it just a coincidence, bad luck? A nasty trick of evolution? Or is it just a matter of a number of cognitive—in the largest sense of the word—biases resulting from evolution's tendency to adapt organisms to a specific environment? Christopher Cherniak, in the article "Limits for Knowledge," suggests that we encounter the limits of our cognitive powers as our investigations of the world take us farther and farther away from the human-size domain of reality, leading us into astrophysical and microphysical realms at a speed much too fast for natural selection to keep up with. "Why," Cherniak asks, "should our cognitive capacities be adequate for all domains, any more than our respiratory capacity can serve on mountain top or ocean floor?"[26] An epistemology that takes for granted that we do know that there is an external world seems to end up with the suggestion that there are fundamental limits for our knowledge. This leads Cherniak to defend the opposite of what he calls the "Peircean, American epistemological optimism—that 'Nature cannot fool all of the investigators all of the time,' i.e., forever."[27] We, and every hominid that may ever have lived, can be wrong. He points out that recent philosophy has tended to overlook such limits for knowledge because of an overidealization of the epistemic agent. Epistemic agents, he contends, do not need to be ideal.

But it appears to me that an even stronger, but at the same time more positive, point needs to be made: Those very limits allow us to function cognitively in the first place. That the limits as we know them, or as we believe we know them, might be "nothing but" perceived limits that do not fully coincide with our "real" limits—as might very well be the case—could only corroborate my point: Not only does the fact that we "only" perceive limits—as opposed to having complete and undistorted knowledge about them—exactly assume the operation of the very limitations that I am referring to, but this also indicates that we can do our work within those limits, that we can use them constructively. Epistemic agents not only do not *need* to be ideal; they *cannot* be perfect, they *cannot* be infinite or ideal. Limitation is a necessary condition for knowledge and also, in a reflexive movement, for the fuzzy (limited) understanding of the limitation itself. Conversely, knowledge is, as such, an indication of our limitation. "La dolce far niente" is not really an option that is available to us. We are not what Kant calls an "intellectus archetypus," an intellect that does not need to experience—in the broadest sense of the word—in order to think and that does not need to think in order to experience: a form of pure knowledge.[28] Such an intellect would not be capable of learning, for there is nothing that it would not already know; it would take no interest in knowledge, for knowing would not be a challenge. Consequently, this being would be completely adapted to every possible world, to every possible environment. Its existence would defy the very concepts of evolution, change, and adaptation. There would be, in other words, no need for evolution. Conversely, limitations are a necessary condition of evolution. The perfect, unlimited, infinite system in principle cannot be evolutionary, because there would be nothing that it could adapt to.

The language of interdisciplinarity can therefore not be the specific language of any of the individual disciplines, as I have argued earlier in this chapter, but neither can it be a language that would "add up" those languages. Such a composite language would defy interdisciplinarity; it would defy language itself, as it would assume the breakdown of the distinctions and the limits that are the very conditions for the existence of knowledge, disciplines, and language. If, in other words, the perspective of all perspectives—the absolute perspective—were possible, perspective as such would no longer be possible.

The very distinction between ontology and epistemology cannot be made without an acceptance of the limitation of both any ontic and any epistemic system. But making that distinction does, therefore, at the same time, mean that we do know something: It means that we know that we are limited and that those limits are a necessary condition for our awareness of that. And to that extent knowledge, *in its origin,* carries self-reference with it, a self-reference that is incomplete or partial. Otherwise, only a complete and closed system could follow from this knowledge, which is obviously not the case.

Chapter 3

The Question Concerning Language

You taught me language, and my profit on't
Is, I know how to curse.
—*Shakespeare,* The Tempest, 1.2

A World of Language

The preliminary analysis in the previous chapter made it quite clear that neither the quest for a single, unified theory nor deconstruction's extreme diversification can provide us with a sound foundation for interdisciplinarity. The world itself is both unified and diversified, and any serious onto-epistemic theory will have to account for those characteristics. In this chapter, I will therefore further investigate the crucial notion of unity in diversity. I will attempt to show how the world itself can be unified in its diversity, and that such a condition is necessary for the existence of the world in the first place. In other words, I will try to show that interdisciplinarity, which focuses on how distinct disciplines have a common ground in the overall structure of the world, is not merely a Derridean language game for which the world is of no relevance and which itself is of no relevance to the world. Interdisciplinarity leads to a fundamental understanding of the world in which we live. As such, it can have significant effects on the future evolution of the world and our symbiotic relation with it.

To set the stage for such an analysis, I want to comment on the specific use of the word *language* in this work as referring to physical events and actions as well as language in the traditional, restricted sense. Language in the traditional sense can be described as that wonderful and attractive mixture of unity and diversity that we also find in nature, in the world in general. Communication requires a common ground—in the form of vocabulary, context, grammatical structure—in order for communication to be possible at all. At the same time, communication also requires enough diversity to make it interesting. What could be the point in talking to somebody who systematically repeats whatever we just said? We might as well talk to a mirror.

Is not biological evolution—our own genetic system, for example—similar in structure to language? Is not chemistry a system in which simple elements combine to form more complex entities that are not simply exact copies of each other? Other examples could be given. The point is that it is tempting to indicate the behavior of parts of the world as "language," not as a mere description but in essence, or at least as a description applying to our human language as well as to the world outside our language. That claim is fundamentally realistic. It does not simply mean that the structure of our language determines our description of the world. It implies, however, that the structure of the world, through the evolutionary processes, determines the structure of our language. I call "language" then, the structure that the world and "our" language have in common. Obviously, our human language and the world do not correspond completely, but that is precisely the point: The relation between our human language and the languages of the world is itself an example of unity in diversity.

But, one might ask, does this not lead us to an ultimately trivial position, to the use of a terminology that can prove everything and which therefore proves nothing at all? Could not just anything be accounted for by such a model, and would that not make the model extremely weak? Does not "language," then, become as abrasive as the Derridean "text," as flat and ungrounded as any endless loop of signs? These questions and remarks can certainly not be discarded as "methodological issues." On the contrary, they go straight to the heart of the matter, for they suggest that the use of the term *language* to describe the general structure of the world might lead up to just another quest for a single formula, namely, language.

A first part of an answer to those questions would point out that the model should indeed explain everything. That may seem an ambitious endeavor, but as we are only presenting a minimal framework, the task at hand really is not that overwhelming. The purpose of the model is not to describe the world in its finest detail. The purpose, rather, is to point at the evolutionary advantages of an overall strategy combined with a great deal of level-specific freedom—a level-specific responsibility that ultimately might go as far as changing or adapting the overall strategy.

This brings us to a second part of a possible answer. The interdisciplinary model, however general, has specific implications that can even be empirically verified. In chapter 4, I discuss how paradoxical events, which threaten the continued existence of the language system, can trigger a level jump—a sudden increase in the complexity of the system. Since no system as rich as our world can be free of paradoxes, level jumps should occur as part of the system's evolution. In other words, a fundamental paradox will necessarily be followed by a level jump. A paradox that is not followed by a jump to a higher level can only point at a dead end on the evolutionary path. The point I want to make at this stage is that differentiation is built into the model as an essential feature. Changing strategies is part of the strategy.

A dramatically enlarged notion of language does not lead to what may seem the disintegration of the specificity of each of the specific levels of complexity involved. What goes on at each of the different levels of reality—in each of the specific languages—is specific and can in principle never be completely reduced to lower levels.

By using the word *language* in an enlarged sense—referring to the minimal structure one can find on every level of reality, in mathematics as well as in quantum physics and so on, and obviously also in our human language—we can avoid the shocking reduction of human language to the level of purely physical events (as the quest for a single unified theory would ultimately imply) as well as the frightful separation of language and world that is implied by deconstruction. A minimal structure of recurrent conditions is the necessary condition for the existence of anything whatsoever. That minimal structure, which I call "language," is therefore the fundamental object of ontology.

Why am I willing to risk a lot of confusion by using "language" as a central notion? Why not consistently use another word instead of *language* to refer to the minimal structure of the world? The answer is simple. It is relatively easy to use a more complex structure (such as our language) to refer to a less complex structure (a chemical reaction, for example), thereby in a sense crediting the less complex with the richness of texture of the higher levels for which it is a condition. The inverse, however—using a less complex structure to describe the more complex—will almost inevitably entail a substantial reduction of the richness of the more complex level. Any term that essentially operates on a level below human language—*event* and *action* are examples thereof—would trigger such a reduction, which would in turn prohibit the essentially interdisciplinary aspect of this project. Life cannot be described exhaustively in terms of physical actions, and to the extent that the physical world is a condition for the coming about of life, that conditional relation between physics and biology cannot be described purely on the physical level.

In other words, I want to make clear that the use of the term *language* in this work is essentially heuristically necessary, given the specific nature of the subject of the research. But such a heuristic condition by no means implies that human language, on the ontic level, somehow prescribes the physical events that are its own existential preconditions. Human language, of course, feeds back into the physical level, just as cultural evolution feeds back into biological evolution. We can verbally structure and create physical experiments without lifting a finger, except to write down some formulas and technical indications. When implemented, these experiments will bring about specific physical events that, for all we know, would never have taken place if it were not for our ability to use "physical language"—that part of our human language that we use to deal with physical events.

The position I defend in this work is that such feedback is possible only because of an essential similarity between "the physical world as language" and our "language of physics." It would be much harder to argue, however, that the "physics of events" is similar to the "event of language." Therefore, although the use of the word *language* as metaphor for the world on all the different levels of complexity on which it exists may at first appear to be somewhat strange and confusing (especially with respect to the Derridean "text"), I believe that it is the most appropriate solution to developing a framework of the fundamental relations and differences among mathematics, physics, chemistry, biology, culture, human language, and so on.

The only inherent restriction to this approach is that the use of the term *language* will appear reductionist with respect to what, eventually, is to come next, after our language. But at the same time this proves my point: The creation of new levels of complexity is essential to the idea that we have a future, that something is ahead of us that is in principle inaccessible to us from the levels on which we exist now. It is only to the extent that we have a past—a mathematical past, a quantum physical past, a chemical past, a biological past, and so on—that we can find out about what is to come next. All those levels that constitute our past have attained some degree of order, confirmed on and by the consequent levels, and it is precisely the stability of the resulting structure of layers of complexity that allows me to "predict" that, in the future, the sun will continue to rise in the East and to set in the West. But such predictions do not concern our future, they concern only our past. As such, any "guaranteed" solution to the problem of world peace that would require the sun to rise in the West can hardly be considered a solution at all. Establishing world peace, on the other hand, will not affect the rising and setting of the sun. As obvious as this may seem, this asymmetry between the cosmological and the political structure is no more self-evident than the world itself. This asymmetry and the conditions thereof are essential to any nontrivial approach of the world in its totality, because they relate to the conditions for the existence of the world itself—for the world of the past as well as for the world of the future.

Our human language, I believe, exists precisely at the crossroad between past and future. Our language has its historical roots in the world, so that the history of the world is the history of our language, and so that the world is language. This work is an attempt to dig into that history of our knowledge, trying to lay bare the roots of the tree of knowledge.

A basic question that provoked much of this project is, Why does language work? Why can we use words to communicate? How can somebody listen to words and then act in response to them? Is there more to language than just our "natural language"?

Almost even more intriguing: Why can we say things that are *wrong*? *Wrong* appears as a violation of some rule applying to how we should use language. Generally speaking, these rules and the restrictions they imply will determine what is wrong and what is correct. If coherency with the world outside human language is such a condition or restriction, then it would follow that any statement that is not coherent with the world is wrong. This approach, also known as the "correspondence theory of truth," is obviously very general and does not indicate how consistency or coherency are to be implemented or verified.

However, looking at these restrictions from a more pragmatic angle, we seem perfectly capable to accept and use them in a broad range of contexts. It may seem fancy or sophisticated to claim that we cannot say things that are wrong because words are just words that are not connected to anything but other words. How could I be *wrong* when playing a game? I could cheat, of course, but could I be wrong? Nevertheless, when somebody tells me that I will get hurt if I jump off a building two-hundred feet high, I know that person is right and that anybody claiming the opposite is wrong. Philosophy too—or maybe *especially* philosophy—has its aberrations: They prove the point I make about our ability to say or express beliefs that are simply wrong.

Words, of course, are related to other words. Signs do refer to other signs. Words do not exist in isolation. When as children we gradually build up a vocabulary, we immediately establish relations, clusters of words. Moreover, there is a substantial number of words that we are not able to define as such: We know and use them only as a part of a larger structure. As a result of the relations among words, we do not need to scan through our complete vocabulary when we want to describe something.

The specific neurobiological wiring of our brain is only part of an explanation of the connections among words. The specific wiring, rather, is an answer to *how* and not to *why*. The answer to the last question can be found only in the relation between the world and our language, a relation that should not be ignored by any theory of language, nor by any theory of the world. In this work, I defend the strongest version of that relation. I argue that we are language; that everything, for that matter, is language. Language is the nature of all being: past, present, and future. *Creation is language. Mathematics is language. Quantum physics is language. Chemistry and biology are language. Human culture is language. Artificial intelligence is—or will be—language.*

I am not referring to the language *of* mathematics, the language *of* physics, and so on. "The language *of* . . ." usually implicitly refers to how we—using human language—talk *about* mathematics, physics, and so on. This leads to the simple, but in the end catastrophic, assertion made by Derrida—"There is nothing but text"—meaning that we have access only to the language we speak and not to the world outside that language. I am referring to the mathematical world *as* language, to the physical world *as* language, and so forth. And I mean these statements to imply that mathematics, physics, and such are *nothing but* language.

The claim that everything is language does not necessarily trivialize language by extending it so much that the concept becomes useless. On the contrary, its implications as I present them in this work reveal the complex and dynamic nature of nature. Again, this is not simply word play. At work here is what I have earlier introduced as a necessary consequence of knowledge, one of the most powerful, and therefore also one of the most dangerous and tricky, aspects of language: self-reference. I suggested that self-reference is a necessary consequence of knowledge and its possibility. Anticipating the next chapters, I want to make the stronger claim that self-reference is an aspect of language as such—in the sense, introduced at the end of chapter 1, that self-reference is ontic and that any ontology, therefore, must be onto-epistemic. Eventually this will lead me to the proposition that knowledge exists on all the levels of reality and not just on the level of human or even biological organisms in general. Even rocks, I will propose, have some form of knowledge about their environment.

My point here, which is also related to the proposition "Everything is language," is that everything in the universe is more similar than it is different. Of course, we are no rocks. But neither are we so different from rocks that our reality is completely cut off from the rock's reality. Between the sixth and the twelfth month of our lives,

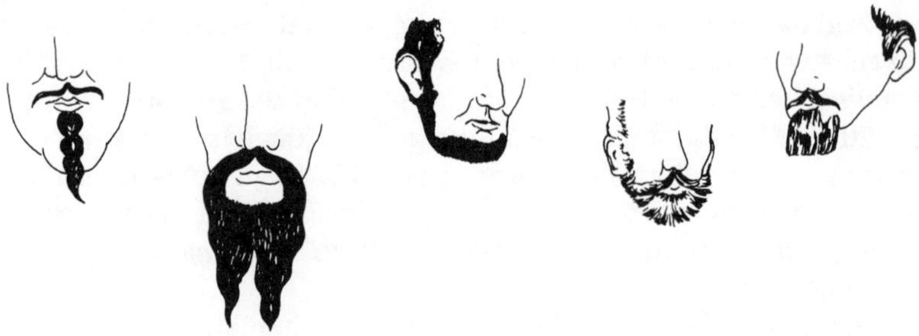

FIGURE 2.
Circle the Differences. In a drawing such as this, the elements are as much similar as different. While no two beards are alike, they nevertheless establish a positive visual relationship among the faces.

we start making a distinction between ourselves and our environment. Until that moment, we do not make such a distinction, although we definitely perceive the world through visual, auditory, and other senses. The accessibility relation between ourselves and the world does not and cannot require an absolute distinction between subject and object. Such a distinction, rather, is influenced by the accessibility relation. A rock has access to the world but cannot distinguish itself from its environment. It cannot construct itself as a separate entity, and therefore it cannot construct itself as an entity at all. Nevertheless, all the understanding of the environment reflects back upon the rock itself. The rock's language is extremely reflexive, in the sense that all of the rock's knowledge relates to the rock itself—what is outside, the "rock-next-door," remains unknown.

Just as we tend to overemphasize distinctions among people because these distinctions stand out so much among all the things people have in common, we tend to stress distinctions between ourselves and the world because we are so much like the rest of the world that we can see only the distinctions that, as I have argued earlier, are a necessary condition for perception, experience, or knowledge to be meaningful at all or even to exist in the first place. (See figure 2.) This does not mean, however, that it is interesting to point at those basic relations in the case of any two particular objects: There is no major point in indicating that on some levels of reality a train is an ironing board as well as a hamburger and a closet—in the sense that on some levels no meaningful distinctions can be made among those objects. A physicist, for that matter, as such cannot distinguish between life and death, between a living creature and a dead object. Those distinctions become meaningful only on the level of biology or biochemistry.

Everything is language is an expression of the basic relations tying together everything that exists, an expression that, because of the very nature of language, leaves enough room for, or even implies, individuality and difference. And this, I believe, is the major premise, the essence, of interdisciplinarity. Interdisciplinarity can exist only on the edge of what connects everything in the universe, on the one hand, and what differentiates everything, on the other. It is a narrow path to walk on.

The Fundamental Structure of Language

Let us try to establish a foundation for the claim that everything is language. The second law of thermodynamics, the entropic principle, states that all organized systems undergo transformations that make them more disorganized. Cybernetics, on the other hand, "the science of maintaining order in a system, whether that system is natural or artificial,"[1] implies an opposite tendency, which can be described as a reaction to entropy, as a continuous correction of the tendency of all things in the world to become entropic or disordered.

The entropic principle, which in the nineteenth century had become a paradigm "predicting" the end of the world, as the universe was supposedly becoming more and more chaotic, found a major application in Shannon's information theory. His chief concern was to establish the mathematics governing information, including a measure of information and a measure of the capacity of a system in general to manipulate that information—store it, send it, receive it, and so on. Shannon treats information as a form of energy, which is, by definition, subject to the entropic principle.

Information is the choice of one message over another. That a light switch can be on or off does not give us much information about the status of the electrical circuit. Once, however, a choice is made between on and off, we receive information, and we then know something about the electrical system. This example, of course, refers to the simplest of choices: a binary choice between yes and no, black and white, on and off. The amount of information available in this choice, a bit, is therefore used as the basic measure of information. Its value is 1, meaning that we have to make just one choice to arrive at an answer. More complex choices can be constructed in terms of this basic unit. Let us assume that we need to choose one of the twenty-six characters of the alphabet. To do that—without taking into account that some characters are more likely to occur than others—we can start by making a choice between the letters *a* through *m* on the one hand and *n* through *z* on the other. This choice will tell us whether the letter we are looking for is in the first or second set of thirteen characters of the alphabet. Continuing this procedure, we can narrow down the choices until we finally come up with the answer. The informative value here, expressed by $\log_2(26)$, equals approximately 4.7, which means that, theoretically, we had to make a choice 4.7 times between two sets of characters of the alphabet in order to come up with the final answer.

The informative value of a message—$H = \log_2(N)$, where N is the number of equally probable messages, or $H = p1 \times \log_2(1/p1) + p2 \times \log_2(1/p2) + \ldots + pn \times \log_2(1/pn)$, where p1, p2, . . . , p*n* are the probabilities assigned to each of the messages 1, 2, . . . , *n* if they are not equally probable—is the same as the entropic value of the message. Shannon's concept of the amount of information and the formula used to arrive at it are the same as the expression of the second principle of thermodynamics, formulated for the first time in the nineteenth century.

Here again we find that basic need for limits imposed on our knowledge. If the entropy or informative value of a message is 0—which means that its probability is 1 and that the probability of all other messages is 0, so that the message is a priori certain—it is no longer possible to speak about information. Information, in other words, can exist only when it is not absolutely certain. Information can exist only when a choice between alternatives, and therefore a probability other than 1, is involved. In a system with no alternatives, in a world with no choices—in a completely deterministic world—information becomes impossible, and the concept meaningless.

The concept of information is obviously closely related to our concept of language, which we can think of as an information system, as a system designed to store, receive, send, and transform information. Cybernetics, on the other hand, which enforces consistency or, given the informal nature of figurative and visual language, coherency, allows for changes, as long as they are not totally random or unstructured. Cybernetics, therefore, which requires at least a partial determinism (in the sense that one can know, for example, that probabilities will indeed govern the behavior of quantum particles) also seems to refer to some of the most fundamental properties of language.

In the 1940s, cybernetics grew out of the combined efforts of Bell Laboratories and MIT to devise an automatic system that would be able to predict—based on initial position, speed, and direction—the position of German airplanes attacking London, so that a correction could be built into the firing of antiaircraft guns. The problem was not easy. Two forms of noise (anything that corrupts the integrity of a message) occurred in the setting: the pilot's attempt to fly as unpredictably as possible and the noise distorting the radar signals. Since it was obviously impossible to influence the behavior of the German pilots, efforts focused on the noise contaminating the radar signal.

Norbert Wiener, at MIT at that time, realized that the seemingly random distortion of the signal was similar to Brownian motion—the behavior of pollen suspended in water, which Einstein showed to be caused by the combined pushes from large numbers of water molecules and to be a quite general phenomenon, not limited just to pollen suspended in water. The mathematics of Brownian motion involve chance and statistics. Wiener started to apply those concepts to the distorted path of an airplane as it was coded in the radar signals, dealing with the path of the airplane as one of many possible paths, just as a piece of information is, in principle, always one of many possible messages.

It may look as if the principles of entropy and cybernetics oppose and even contradict each other. Yet the validity of neither concept seems questionable. Both legitimately claim universality. Cybernetics, in Campbell's words, "is a universal principle of control, and can be applied to all kinds of organization, just as Shannon's theorems apply to communication of all kinds. It does not matter whether the system is electrical, chemical, mechanical, biological, or economic."[2] Here we come as close to a foundation of "Everything is language" as we can, introducing language as the combination of the entropic and the cybernetic. Language, as I try to show in this work, exists exactly at the crossroad of a universal tendency toward order and a universal tendency toward disorder.

If we accept that both information and cybernetics are universal in the sense that they apply to all kinds of organizations—as has been shown sufficiently in the work of Shannon, Wiener, and many others—we must then accept that language itself is universal and thus ontic. Taking this one step further brings us to "Everything is language," meaning that everything exists at the crossroad of a tendency toward order and a tendency toward disorder. Only at such an intersection are existence and knowledge possible: The crossroad between order and disorder is a fundamental onto-epistemic condition.

Shannon's theory of information is syntactic in the sense that it is in principle independent of the meaning of the messages involved. The informative value of *You die* is the same as the informative value of *You live. The universe is left-handed* has no more informative value than *The universe is right-handed.* Information theory, of course, takes into account the fact that one choice occurs more often than another and assigns different probabilities to each of the options. But information theory does not tell us how these probabilities should be assigned, and it tells us even less about why not all probabilities are equal in the first place.

Morton Kaplan introduces correlative concept pairs—"pairs, the meaning of each of which involves the other"—as the basic unit of the semantics of our language.[3] Nothing, for example, is, *as such,* in essence light or dark. *Light* and *dark* depend for their meaning upon each other and a context. If we take his work beyond its intended scope, Kaplan's theory of semantics appears as a special case of Shannon's information theory, a case in which additional conditions are imposed on the relation between the choices that are the basis of the possibility of information.

These additional conditions concern the positive and negative feedback between each of the choices. The distinction between positive and negative feedback can be illustrated by their effects on the choice between VHS and Beta as the format for videocassettes, on the one hand, and the choice between coal and water to generate electricity, on the other.[4] VHS and Beta started out as competitors with an equal market share. In such a situation, even a small increase in sales of one format would encourage video stores to focus on prerecorded tapes in that format, which would in turn lead more people to buy that particular format. It so happened that VHS had that initial edge, even though literature suggests that Beta was technically speaking the better solution. A small initial fluctuation in the market share, due to luck, corporate policy, advertisement, and so on, accumulated because of positive feedback, until VHS virtually took over the whole market. The analysis of these mechanisms is fairly recent in economic theory, which has primarily focused on the effects of negative feedback. When hydroelectric power plants become more and more important in the energy market, the cost associated with them increases as the "easy" locations become less and less available and more costly dams need to be built. At some point the cost of building hydropower plants will exceed that of coal-fired plants, which will then become more likely to be built. But that will increase the demand for coal and therefore increase the price for coal and the cost related to pollution control. In this case, the two technologies will interact in such a way that they will end up with a market share reflecting the potential of both.

Positive and negative feedback link information theory to chaos theory, which essentially deals with the amplifying effects of positive feedback, and to cybernetics, which deals with the regulating effect of negative feedback. These conditions, which I will analyze in the next chapter as being the result of the reflexivity of language, introduce meaning on all levels of reality. Order and chaos, in a reflexive movement of this prototypic correlative pair, make the world meaningful in all its aspects, on all its levels—levels that, as I will argue, are the result of this reflexive movement.

Order in chaos—"science's oldest cliché," as James Gleich puts it. Physicist Leo Kadanoff was, together with Kenneth Wilson—who would later refine the mathematical aspect of Kadanoff's work—one of the important ancestors of chaos theory. His research on phase transitions established a backbone for the relation between transitions on different, seemingly unrelated levels: the boiling of liquids, the magnetizing of metals, and so on. Kadanoff was puzzled by the problem of how each of the small pieces of a metal block could make the same decision about the orientation of the magnetic field when the metal block is magnetized. His fundamental contribution consists of the insight that a fundamental relation exists between communication and information, on the one hand, and scaling, on the other.

Information exists on different scales and can be understood only in relation to a specific scale. This strikingly resembles the way in which information is contained in our human verbal language, but also, as I claim in this work, in language in general. When we look at a text, at a book for example, we can ask ourselves where exactly its information is hidden. We seemingly deal with a flat object, a thin layer of ink on a thin layer of paper. But a closer look, from whichever epistemic point of view, will reveal different levels on which the text exists: its material substance, the level of the alphanumeric signs, the levels of morphemes, words, phrases and clauses, sentences, paragraphs, chapters, the book, and even beyond, on the level of the culture in which the book was produced. Where then do we find the meaning of the text? It is nowhere and everywhere. It is not possible to point at one single level and say, "Look, here we find the information, here we find what this text is about." The meanings of words, as Miller and Johnson-Laird put it, "must be compatible with the meanings of sentences. Procedures for constructing sentences and interpreting them must dovetail with procedures representing the meanings of words."[5]

A similar requirement, we might add, can be imposed on the relation between all the levels on which the language exists. Not only do we have to look at all the levels involved when we want to understand our language and how it functions, but at the same time we cannot look at a text and leave out any of the levels on which it exists. We cannot read a text while ignoring, consciously or unconsciously, any of its layers. At least not, that is, without substantially distorting the information contained in it. It would be like taking all the lines out of a painting or looking at a sculpture without being able to see the material out of which it was made.

The only way to reduce the number of levels is to translate one language into another language that has a less complex structure. But when we do so, we are at risk of losing or reducing another important feature of information and its communication: redundancy. The different levels on which a text exists provide the information with a certain redundancy needed for error-free communication. When I make a mistake on any of the levels, a spelling mistake, for example, or when I leave out a word, that mistake will usually be recognized as such and corrected by the other levels. In fact, this is a clear indication that the information is present on all levels at the same time and not on just one of them.

If our language were a flat object—a single layer, so to speak—such a flexibility would be impossible, since no criterion would exist to make a distinction between a mistake and a false or even nonsensical sentence. We would no longer be able to make such distinctions either within language or within the relation between our language and the world. In other words, if our language were a flat object, not only would communication be highly improbable, but it would also be improbable that language refers to the world.

A similar, although much more simple, form of the redundancy that exists within the layered structure of our language can be found in the number of words in a telegram added at the end of the message, providing a rough criterion to evaluate the accuracy of the transmission. Another example would be the bit added at the end of a binary-coded piece of information—namely, 1 if all the other bits of the information add up to an uneven number, or 0 if they add up to an even number. Here again a simple tool is created to evaluate the transmission. These redundant numbers, however, do not code the message itself. In other words, they cannot be substituted for the message. Once an error is detected by means of such simple forms of redundancy, it can be corrected only by sending the original message again. On the other hand, if the complexity of the redundancy is increased and more cross-references are added, the message will ultimately become self-healing. Corrections can then be made without going back to the original source.

But what about the levels of reality? What about the levels of physics, chemistry, biology, culture, and so forth, on which we can describe the world? Are these levels, too, just a matter of redundancy with respect to the basic level of complexity, or do they add to the original message? Or should we look at it as follows: that something new is created in the process of adding redundancy? These questions bring us back to the problem of interdisciplinarity.

To a large extent disciplines can be described by the terminology they use, by their private and highly specialized language. To become knowledgeable in a field implies, in the first place, mastering that field's terminology as established in a large number of discipline-specific dictionaries and reference books. However, terminology is more than just a way to determine the extent of a discipline. Terminology has definite epistemological implications. It is therefore important, as Arthur Miller points out, to assume that scientists such as Bohr, Einstein, or Heisenberg would choose their words carefully when writing a paper. Miller asserts that "the shifts in the meanings of certain terminologies in their scientific papers and correspondence signal transformations of physical reality."[6] Miller's position is a strong one, but I believe that it refers to the only acceptable hypothesis about why our language works in the first place. It is in essence a position that assumes the existence of a fundamental relation between our language and the world. The importance of that position can hardly be overestimated, since much more is at stake here than just the professional integrity of scientists and philosophers. At stake here is the possibility of making a distinction between good and bad, between right and wrong, between true and false. At stake here are knowledge, art, ethics, beauty.

Derrida's crossing out of words—his *sous rature*—is simply not acceptable and should fool nobody, not even himself. Derrida cannot write without using words. Intended to be "the mark of the absence of a presence, an always already absent present, of the lack at the origin that is the condition of thought and experience,"[7] *sous rature* is anything but that. It is the real presence of the world in our language that is the fundamental epistemic condition, the condition of thought and experience. Without that condition, true and false no longer exist, as they themselves are erased and cannot be recovered. *True* and *false* become interchangeable, and in the end it no longer matters what we choose to say.

Language has then become a game, a language game. Wittgensteinian in origin, this terminology has been picked up by Derrida to indicate the endless reference of signs to other signs. But, of course, a game has to be played according to rules, according to limits imposed on possible moves. In other words, a game, in order to be played, must have the characteristics that Derrida denies the world.

And who is going to decide on the rules? Are all games equally probable and valid? Of course not, but even if they are, not all games are being played. Somehow a selection has to be made: Not all games are equally interesting.

The endless loop of references among signs leads to a situation of maximal entropy, where all the words or all the messages have the same probability. In such a system, as in a system in which only one absolutely certain message exists, information cannot exist: What at first appears to be a choice between an endless number of possibilities turns out to be the opposite. No real choice can be made, since no grounds on which a decision—any decision—could be made, can be established. Instead of contributing to the cybernetic reintroduction of order, a "choice" within such a system will only contribute to the increase of the entropy of the system. The feedback between the signs is never positive, as in cybernetics, but is rather completely indifferent to the system, because under such conditions there simply is no system. The endless reference among signs does not add to the complexity of language, but makes it increasingly impossible for language to be meaningful—nontrivial—at all.

Distinct Languages

Although I have identified the problem of interdisciplinarity as a problem of language, the answer cannot be found in linguistics, which, as I see it, has the specific conditions of human language as its subject. Language, according to Chomsky, is a "mirror of the mind," meaning that our use of language should give us a better understanding of unconscious knowledge. Understanding the nature of the human mind then becomes Chomsky's goal for linguistics. Within the tradition of Zellig Harris, under whom he studied at the University of Pennsylvania, Chomsky attempts to deal with a language that is stripped of any meaning beyond syntax, stripped of any relation with a world outside language. The only external relation that Chomsky admits is one between the (innate) deep structure of language and the structure of the human mind. Such a linguistic approach to language, however valuable and heuristically important, can never answer the fundamental questions, such as, Why does language work, or Why do we need language in the first place? At most, it will be able to establish some of the mechanisms, the syntax that allows language to be the powerful tool that it definitely is.

But if the answer to the problem of the language of interdisciplinarity is not linguistics, then neither is it any other science dealing with language on a specific level—be it physics, biology, chemistry, or any other discipline. Quantum physics, for example, is not chemistry. And yet, if we claim that both are language, then both should share at least a minimal—ontic—structure.

We could say that physics and chemistry are both languages in much the same way as French and English are. But this parallel holds only to some extent. Although French and English cannot be translated completely into each other, nobody would claim that French and English refer to different worlds, to different realities, to different levels of reality. They exist parallel to each other. Not so with quantum physics and chemistry. We can reasonably claim that we would not have chemistry without quantum physics, while the inverse position is much harder to defend: Quantum physics does not necessarily entail chemistry.

But, one might ask, what about the Eskimo's many words to indicate snow? Does the Eskimo live in a different world than we do, in a world with several sorts of snow as opposed to our world with just one variety? Yet if we would look at the world very carefully, we might be able to distinguish between more than just one type of snow, which we can more or less accurately describe by using adjectives or by telling a story that reminds us of the mood associated with a specific type of snow. Through scientific observation, with the use of tools and mathematical formulae to describe the forms and shapes of snow, we might even discover that there is much more to snow than even the Eskimo can express in his or her language. On its own level of complexity, on its own level of existence, snow, when pointed at by somebody, is certainly not different when pointed at by somebody else. It is just that our conscious human participation at that level is relatively minimal and forces us to gain access to that level of reality through a translation or projection of its language into our own language—human language.

The strong relation between words and the world is the basis of Wittgenstein's "reduction" of language to "pointing at the world." Unless we agree to accept a solipsistic perspective—which is no perspective at all, because it does away with the onto-epistemic distance between ourselves and the world—we have to accept that the relation between language and perception is a crucial one: We have access to the world (or the world has access to us, if one would prefer to put it that way) through our sensory system. Perception is what allows us to point at the world in the first place. This is reflected in the history of our language, as is clear from the rather successful attempts, initiated by V. Gordon Childe in 1926 in his book *The Aryans*, to locate the origins of Indo-European languages by looking at archaeological evidence for the "core" words for plants and animals, or by looking for the mountainous landscape that is described by the reconstructed Indo-European protolanguage with its abundant vocabulary for mountains, mountain lakes, rapid rivers, and other natural phenomena.[8]

The information resulting from the accessibility relation between epistemic organisms like ourselves and the world is crucial for deciding some of the pragmatic questions involved in determining the value of propositions expressed in language, as in a sentence like *The cat sits on the mat*. The listener or reader has to perceive the specific cat and the specific mat to which reference is made.

In the case of figurative language, however, the language construction often, although not always, makes it clear that perception is not a necessary condition for the understanding of the text. Nevertheless, in that case, too, the language will have to be linked to the world at some point in the cluster of relations among words generated by the figurative language.

Another case where perception is apparently not imposed as a pragmatic condition on the functioning of language includes (analytic) propositions such as *Two is the only even prime number.* But here, too, a relation with the world is established or implicitly assumed to exist. If we claim the universal validity of analytic statements, then these should also hold for the world outside our language. In a language completely cut off from the world, as is Derrida's, there is no place for analytic or synthetic propositions, as the terms *analytic* and *synthetic* apply only if a reference to a world outside our language exists. The analytic proposition, in other words, must be true in the world. Therefore it seems that if we cannot "perceive" the validity of this proposition in the world—we cannot point at the number two and "perceive" that specific number as the only even prime number in the world—we have at least added something to the world: We have added a true statement to the world. To be able to do so, we definitely need to have access to the world, access based on and guaranteed by our being a part of the world.

In general, it is quite obvious that in all these cases where seemingly no pragmatic condition is imposed on the functioning of language, we do have to assume the existence of a strong relation between language and the world. Without such a strong relation, it is hard to understand how our language in all its aspects is to function in a cognitively meaningful way.

Language as Knowledge

Epistemological relativism has taken Gödel's work to unacceptable conclusions, claiming that all knowledge is ultimately impossible. Obviously, this is nonsense. I know that I will get hurt jumping off a five-story building. I know that I need food and water in order to survive, just as I know that I will not live forever. I even know that the odds are against there being no major nuclear disaster between now and eternity.

I know these things, and I know that knowledge, as I have argued, is a form of language. But what language? Is it a form of English? A form of a verbal language, perhaps? Is it even possible, we could ask, to express this knowledge in a nonverbal language?

Attempts have been made to bring science and art closer together by showing that science's actual methodology—in the productive, creative phase—is not so different from what goes on in the creation of a work of art. Thomas Kuhn's concept of "paradigm shift" has been, and still is, fundamental to that attempt. Scientists often use the metaphor of perception when discussing the evolution of a specific theory or even the evolution of science as a whole. According to them, it is just a matter of changing the perspective, changing the angle from which to look at a problem. Each new perspective brings new aspects of the problem to life, and ultimately a coherent image arises in much the same way as a more coherent image of the world arises from the different perspectives presented by artists throughout the history of art. Although there is definitely a certain order, a certain internal logic or chronology, in the sequence in which perspectives—or, for that matter, paradigms—follow each other, it is hard to claim that any of the perspectives is wrong.

If science, or art, does not lead to definite results based on a specific perspective, one should not blame the perspective, according to Kuhn. What has happened, rather, is that not enough different points of view have been explored to present a more or less complete image, a more or less complete understanding of whatever problem or whatever part of the world is the subject of the investigation. Later, Kuhn seems to have somewhat changed his views, admitting there may be grounds to prefer one paradigm over another based on such values as accuracy, consistency, simplicity, and scope. Still, reference to the world is not a core concept in his approach.

The Western epistemological tradition has been dominated by the idea that knowledge is our most valuable asset, even leading to a defination of humanity in terms of a preferred relation that we believe to exist between us and the world we live in. If we want to investigate the vast field of epistemology that lies between us—or any other epistemic organism—and the world, we will have to investigate how we interact with the world, how we base our actions on our perception or understanding, and how our actions—including the act of knowledge!—change the world. This obviously implies that it is no longer possible to subscribe to either of the one-directional views on knowledge: Our knowledge (but also the knowledge of any other organism in the world) is not solely determined by the world, nor are we completely imposing an imaginary structure upon the world.

The first hypothesis, that our knowledge is a true image of the world, has lost its influence, even in the so-called hard sciences like physics, since it is no longer obvious that the different basic elements of the most fundamental theories (quarks, gluons, leptons, etc.) refer to real entities, to "objects." But as a result of this, the second hypothesis, that we impose a structure on the world, has significantly gained momentum, leading to a strange epistemological perspective that can be characterized by two hierarchies operating simultaneously.

First of all, we basically express knowledge in a verbal structure. Other media, particularly the visual media, are then used to support this verbal structure or to make the headlines easily (literally, at a glance) accessible. As the implicit argument goes, a picture is indeed worth a thousand words, but the words are where the meaning is. And indeed, computers become more and more graphical, but that is just a matter of a user interface, it is just a matter of an overlay to make the real thing, the rigid hardware and its language of currents, more easily accessible.

Under the conditions of this first hierarchy, images submit themselves to a supposedly superior, verbal structure. As Lindekens puts it in his *Essai de sémiotique visuelle:* "Just as dreams come to even the most strictly secluded young girls, words end up living in images, whether we like it or not, and they sometimes even end up masking what are their most subversive and unrestrained qualities. At that point we probably should admit that images cannot have a full meaning without a more or less explicit contribution of the word."[9] This is basically the idea behind "In the beginning was the Word"—the word of the Bible in particular, but also the words of the corpus of religious texts. We find this, for instance, in *L'Évangile des pauvres* inside Notre-Dame in Paris, where the text of the gospel has been "depicted" in order to make it accessible to the illiterate. The subversive and unrestrained qualities that a visual image can express have been removed as far as possible: Everything is constructed according to a conventional system that simply mirrors the verbal structure. The image is read as if it were a text. Consequently, what we cannot read disappears from the image.

These are just a few examples of the diverse forms taken on by this first hierarchy, which explicitly claims the superiority of verbal language over visual images. In general, this hierarchy seems to some extent related to the hypothesis that we impose a structure on the world, to the idea that we more or less arbitrarily build up networks of words that are, at best, only locally linked to what is going on in the world.

The second hierarchy has to do with literal versus discursive language. Literal statements—and, as a result of the impact of the first hierarchy, especially literal verbal statements—are often considered to refer directly to the world, and a higher truth value is therefore attributed to them. We find this, for instance, in an extreme form in the fundamentalist interpretation of the Bible, which denies any kind of truth, or even any kind of cognitive value, to a figurative reading. This second hierarchy appears to be closely related to the idea that our knowledge—when expressed in the right form and medium—consists of an adequate image of the world.

It seems to me that the cognitive priority of verbal discursive language is in some strange way the result of a combination of both hierarchies, leading to a position where a specific—literal and verbal—mode of reference to the world is identified with reference to the world as such. This position, in other words, identifies the literal aspect of language with its denotative aspect.

Quine, a perfect example of this tendency, describes metaphor as vital at the growing edges of science and philosophy, but ultimately considers this as just practice for the real stuff. Metaphor, or figurative language in general, is essential to the growth and acquisition of language, but, as Quine puts it, "the neatly worked inner stretches of science are an open space in the tropical jungle, created by clearing the tropes away."[10] His position is even more evident when he answers the question why religion is so dependent upon metaphor:

> Exegete succeeds exegete, ever construing metaphor in further metaphor. There are deep mysteries here. There is mystery as to *the literal content, if any, that this metaphorical material is meant to convey.* And there is then a second-order mystery: Why the *indirection*? If the message is as urgent and important as one supposes, why are we not given it straight in the first place? A partial answer to both questions may lie in the nature of mystical experience: *it is without content and so resists literal communication,* but one may still try to induce the feeling in others by skillful metaphor.[11]

Even though this is a short passage, it contains numerous assumptions about the relation between literal and figurative language that illustrate my point about the hierarchical relation between the literal and the figurative in the Western epistemological tradition. Metaphor is meant to convey literal content. Metaphor is indirect. Literal language is the appropriate language for what is urgent and important. What is ironical in this whole situation is, of course, that while a fundamentalist interpretation of the Bible presents the metaphors as literal language, Quine actually almost blames the metaphors for not being literal. Quine and the fundamentalists at least agree about the primacy of literal language. According to Quine, the lack of content (read: the absence of reference to the world) makes the use of literal language almost impossible, because literal language is par excellence the language of reference. Indeed, Quine grants metaphor an important position as a prerequisite of literal language, but ultimately his point is not so different from the one presented by logical positivism: Metaphor is useful but one should not make cognitive claims for it.

I believe that in accepting this dual hierarchy and the identification of denotation with literal verbal language, we unnecessarily—and, as can be argued, even fatally—restrict our possible knowledge about the world. The verbal and the nonverbal, the discursive and the figurative, cannot be reduced to one another, even when they ultimately refer to the same world.

Why should figurative language be impossible without the aid of a literal, verbal meaning? When we assume that our language refers to the world, it seems useless to construct the figurative based on the literal or even as a deviation of the literal. Even the assumption that figurative language functions as a shortcut for discursive language—exactly as visual language is supposed to be a shortcut for verbal language!—does not make much sense, then, and definitely contradicts our experience with language. It is only when language is no more than a game with its own rules for which the world is irrelevant that it seems necessary to construct the figurative as a specific case of the literal, since otherwise the figurative would loose every reference and become meaningless and trivial. Unless, of course, we want to accept—but why should we?—that we are playing two language games simultaneously, that we are playing according to two different sets of rules.

The same remarks also hold for nonverbal forms of knowledge. Why should nonverbal knowledge be meaningful only in relation to verbal knowledge? Here the argument is even stronger, since the direct relation between the visual and the world is even more stringent than the relation between a verbal structure and the world. It is easier to accept that a visual language refers to the world in a cognitively meaningful way, since our experience of images is—even in the case of an abstract painting—more closely related to our experience of the environment in which we live. Most people do not believe that a word as such is an image of the world or of something in the world, whereas most people will readily accept that the pictures they take are real images of the things out there, or that an abstract painting contains to some extent the same qualities as the objects in the world.

The point that a nonverbal language adds something to a verbal language should be made not only with respect to visual and verbal language but also with respect to other types of languages—auditory, kinesthetic, tactile, and so on. Dane Harwood recounts in *Music Cognition* how at one point she joined a musical ensemble whose purpose was to play Javanese gamelan instruments. She was assigned a *gong ageng*—a large gong that supposedly was the easiest instrument to play, as it was used only a couple of times in every piece they performed. Nevertheless, the native Indonesian musicians in the ensemble continued to point out to her that often her timing was off: Even if formally correct, it was not always appropriate to strike the gong exactly at the beat. "Over time," she recounts, "I came to understand that manner of striking was important and that tempo, musical genre, and even the acoustic characteristics of the individual gong determined how and precisely when it should be played."[12]

Music and verbal language have many elements in common. Dowling and Harwood point out that our verbal and musical behavior undoubtedly evolved hand in hand. They share systems for perceptual analysis and vocal production, as well as more elaborate temporal control systems in the brain.[13] Regardless of that common basis, the native musicians were never able to verbally account for the phenomenon or to express verbal rules that could be followed. However, all of them were able to consistently demonstrate the "right" sound and timing, and these performances were clearly appreciated and preferred by the audience. Dowling and Harwood qualify this type of knowledge, which also applies to Western European music, as "implicit," "tacit," "not bounded by the explicitly verbalized or by textbooks on music theory."[14]

I believe that a much stronger claim can be made: that we are dealing with an auditory language, or, more precisely, with that part of auditory language that escapes the constraints of verbal language and that can therefore in principle never be completely expressed in verbal language.

The obvious question is whether these irreducible nonverbal elements—visual, auditory, or other—indeed have a cognitive value of their own or whether they are just cognitively redundant features that are of no relevance to the semantic functioning of language, except, maybe, for adding to our pleasure when we look at a painting or listen to music. This matter is important, because this problem ultimately refers to the question of whether or not there is a point in having distinct languages, be it verbal and nonverbal languages or languages that relate to distinct disciplines.

To illustrate my affirmative answer to that question, I would like to present an example of the extremely powerful tool that is created by the integration of, or cooperation between, verbal and visual language, in particular between figurative verbal and visual language. A number of years ago I discovered, almost by accident, that some dyslexic children display a higher than average sensibility to the semantics of visual language. One young man with definite and apparently insurmountable problems related to reading, writing, arithmetic, a linear time structure, and other cognitive processes turned out to have a very rich understanding of visual language (in painting, architecture, etc.) even though it was very hard for him to verbalize that understanding. Later—too late, since for years his problems had been interpreted as related to the fact that he had been living in a completely different culture until he was five or six years old—when he was diagnosed as severely dyslexic, I started looking into the possibility for him to use visual language as a way to compensate for some of the problems he experienced in verbal language.

Dyslexia, over the last couple of years, has become a fashionable "disorder." Although the problem is certainly real, dyslexia has become something like a cognitive flu: It does not imply that you are stupid, but it explains that you are performing below your "real" potential. In *DSM-III-R* (the *Diagnostic and Statistical Manual of Mental Disorders, Third Edition, Revised,* published by the American Psychiatric Association), dyslexia is not diagnosed as such. In the index, reference is made to Developmental Reading Disorder. This disorder is part of the group Specific Developmental Disorders, more specifically of Academic Skills Disorders. These disorders have in common that, first of all, the skills involved are definitely below the expected level based on schooling and overall intelligence—they are, in other words, not caused by mental retardation or deficient educational opportunities. Secondly, that the deficient skills interfere with academic performance and/or daily routine involving the specific skill. Finally, that they are not due to a neurological disorder or a sensory impairment. The group Specific Developmental Disorders also includes Language and Speech Disorders, Coordination Disorders, and Specific Developmental Disorder Not Otherwise Specified. I will not engage in a detailed discussion of how those disorders affect each other, nor of the alternative classifications that have been suggested, but the reader should realize that we are dealing with a complex set of overlapping problems. Rarely does one find a "patient"—which, I believe, is not a pertinent qualification, because it implies a medical model—who can be diagnosed for only one of the disorders listed in *DSM-III-R*. Consistent with the way in which the term has been used, or misused, in the past, I will continue to use *dyslexia* in general as referring to any combination of the specific disorders mentioned here, including the disorder concerning the understanding of figurative verbal language.

What is essential to the point I am trying to make is that similar problems related to nonverbal language or subjects other than mathematics are not explicitly included in *DSM-III-R*, unless, of course, under trash-category 315.90, Specific Developmental Disorder Not Otherwise Specified. The question is, why? Is it, maybe, because the problem simply does not exist in domains not included in *DSM-III-R?* It is possible, of course, that no visual or other nonverbal counterpart for dyslexia exists, but the fact remains that dyslexia and related problems often involve the visual and auditory qualities of verbal language. I therefore assume that the flagrant absence of any reference to nonverbal language in *DSM-III-R* does not mean that the problem does not exist in nonverbal language, but rather that it goes unnoticed because we do not teach students to use visual language. Nobody in his or her right mind will call a baby "language impaired." The baby still needs to learn how to use language; it is only later that a lagging verbal ability can be noticed. Since most of us never learn how to use nonverbal languages like drawing or painting, it is only normal that problems related to those languages go unnoticed—unless, of course, we accept that most people have severe problems with nonverbal language and that painters, musicians, and other artists are the "normal" people.

During my research about how dyslexic children can use visual language to overcome some of the problems they have with verbal language, I came across several remarkable cases of children with a specific language comprehension impairment that makes it virtually impossible for them to understand or use figurative verbal language.

As a result of this impairment, they fundamentally restrict themselves to the literal use of verbal language, thereby restricting their ability to use knowledge in one discipline as a basis for knowledge in another field by transferring it metaphorically. In some cases, this even included the inability to transpose rules for behavior from one environment to another.

When asked to visualize and actually draw the figurative verbal language, some of the children with the figurative-verbal language disorder were able to solve most of the semantic problems occurring in the verbal language. It did not stop there: Quite often they added on to the semantic structure that is expected to be contained in or expressed by the strictly verbal language. In other words, they were able to create a much richer semantic frame than "normal" children. The overlapping between the different types of languages even allowed them to get back to verbal language and deal with the figurative aspects of it in a way that at first had been impossible.

Such an overlapping among the different languages is crucial, because it is within this intersection that the notion of coherency can be used to evaluate the different perspectives we get when using different media, different languages. It turned out, namely, that after the children had obtained a more or less adequate understanding through the use of (in the case of this study) a visual language, they immediately tended to change the contents of their verbal understanding in order to gain coherence with the visual understanding.

What follows now are transcriptions of typical conversations that went on during the process of using visual language to get around problems with verbal language. Philippe, who made these particular drawings, was at that time eleven years old. His developmental background includes a period of six months of elective mutism at ages three and four, in his case related to a systematic exposure to a second language, which, after the period of silence, he was perfectly able to speak. His intelligence is definitely above average, even when measured in verbal tests. He was diagnosed as dyslexic at the age of seven and had since been enrolled in a special program for dyslexic children. I hear that he recently changed back to a traditional system and that he is doing extremely well.

Philippe systematically tends to a literal interpretation of figurative verbal language and is surprised when figurative language is explained to him. His limited ability to deal with figurative verbal language in everyday life is based on memorizing reductive discursive definitions that have been a substantial part of his remedial program.

The first drawing deals with the figurative expression, *a vein of gold,* which has become such a standard expression that we just take its meaning for granted. Although he perfectly understood the words *gold* and *vein,* Philippe could at first not even suggest a possible meaning for *a vein of gold,* which is a strong indication of its irreducibly figurative semantic structure.

To make his drawing, Philippe disposed of about twenty different color markers. It took him about five minutes to draw the outline of a human body with a red heart and a number of red and blue veins leading from the heart to the arms, the legs, and the head. Then he added one yellow "vein" leading from the heart to one of the legs. (See figure 3.)

KDP: And now, what do you think a vein of gold is?

Ph.: Well, you know, from your heart you have two different veins, with blue and red blood. But I am not sure what the difference is. But maybe a vein of gold is a very special vein with something different in it.

KDP: Do we have gold in our bodies?

Ph.: No, of course not.

KDP: Where can you find gold?

Ph.: (silence) Oh, now I get it. A vein of gold is like something that brings gold from the heart of the earth to all different places where we can find it.

Philippe had not only fully understood the meaning of *a vein of gold,* but he added a dynamical context to the rather static interpretation that "normal" children come up with. On top of that, he was able to create an analogous metaphor, *heart of the earth,* in his effort to express his understanding verbally. That is significant, because it indicates that metaphor, like other types of figurative speech, is indeed not a local shortcut for discursive language, but that a specific metaphor is part of a larger network of figurative speech—in the same way as the word *table* not only refers to a specific object but also hints at a larger context (chair, dinner, etc.).

The next example deals with the expression *This child is a rose.* Although this too has become a standard expression, it has, for obvious reasons, maintained a somewhat more poetic status than *a vein of gold.*

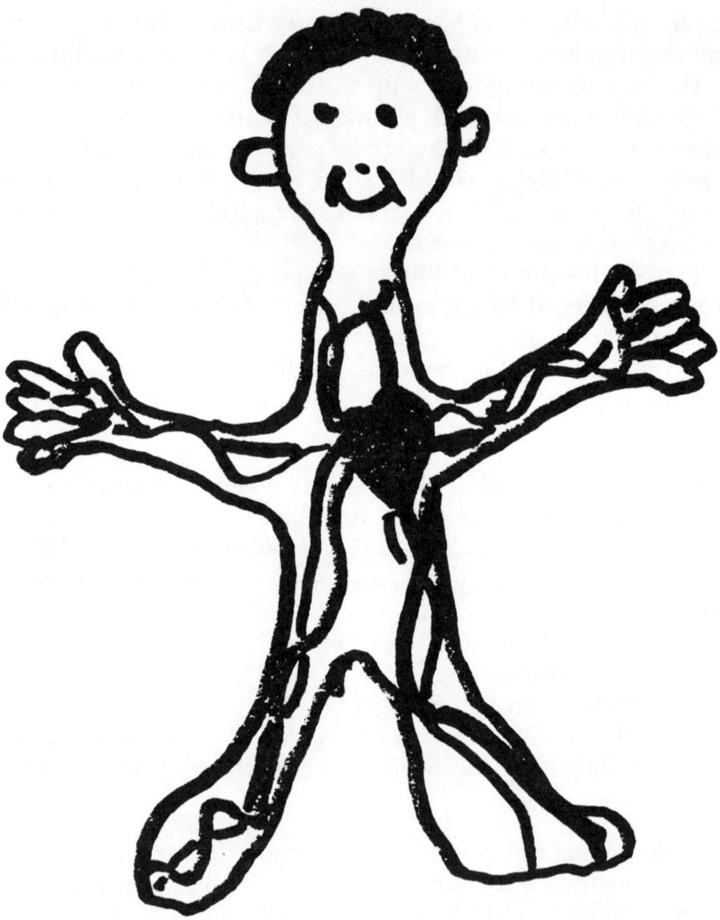

FIGURE 3.
A Vein of Gold. The figurative core of this expression makes it hard to deal with for people with an impaired understanding of figurative verbal language. A shift toward visual language may help to overcome the problem.

KDP: When I say "This child is a rose," what does that mean?

Ph.: This child is a beautiful thing. Wait. Hm . . . that the child is picky.

KDP: What has that to do with a rose?

Ph.: Because it has thorns on it.

FIGURE 4.
This Child Is a Rose. The elements of the drawing are embedded in a larger context—a landscape. As such, a permanent but dynamic set of hot-links is established between the visual elements.

KDP: What else?
Ph.: Does it all has to be focused on one child?
KDP: No, in general.
Ph.: It can also mean an mean person, or a mad person.
KDP: A mad person?
Ph.: Yes, a mad person.

At that point, I asked Philippe to make a drawing about the expression *This child is a rose.* (See figure 4.)

Ph.: Can I do like a child with a very red face? Would that be good?
KDP: That could be a start.

Philippe draws a green human figure with a red face, wearing a shirt scattered with green dots. The feet of the figure are roots that disappear under the ground. In the upper right corner he draws a sun and two small clouds. The horizon is bent upward to the sun.

KDP: Tell me about the drawing.
Ph.: Here is this . . . the face is the top of the flower. The hair and the ears (he adds the ears while saying this) are like the blossom.

And then, his arms are the stem. I messed up this part. (He points at the green blot on the shoulder of the figure.) The green dots are thorns.

KDP: What else do you have in your drawing?

Ph.: Then it still the stem, and the feet are roots. And this is a landscape and it is going up to show that it goes on.

KDP: When you look at your drawing, and I ask you what it means to say "This child is rose" . . .

Ph.: It is a beautiful child.

KDP: A beautiful child? Something else?

Ph.: It is a nice child.

KDP: What about what you told me before, that it means "a bad child"?

Ph.: I didn't really get the definition then.

KDP: Would you still hold on to what you told me then?

Ph.: . . .

KDP: Or would you change it?

Ph.: Change it.

KDP: What would be changed? What is different?

Ph.: I would say that it is a beautiful child, a nice child?

KDP: Yes, but why would you no longer say that it is a bad child, or a picky child—as you called it?

Ph.: A rose is a beautiful thing. And most beautiful things have been growing up very good. And they don't go (changes his voice to a higher pitch) "Oh, mammy, can I do this or this?"

Although Philippe seemingly started off where he would ultimately end up—that *This child is a rose* means *This is a beautiful child*—a major difference in his understanding took place while he went through the process of visual thinking. In the beginning of the process, before he made the drawing, he abandoned "This child is beautiful thing" almost immediately in favor of a more specific relation between thorns and being picky. The general characterization, which he had presumably picked up somewhere, was less tangible for him than the immediate, almost physical connection with the thorns. Since I wanted him to make the drawing, I could not really press him on this issue, but on other occasions, when I continued to ask him for "more" verbal understanding, he simply went from one characteristic to another and adapted his definition of the expression accordingly. When he was cued about some of the properties of the sun (light, heat, beach, desert), his interpretation of *You are my sunshine* simply shifted along with the respective implications.

It seems as if, during and after the process of visual thinking, Philippe has simultaneous access to all the features of the rose (features that he has carefully included in his drawing) but also to features of "child" (remember how he added the ears while talking about the drawing) and their common environment, the landscape that he explicitly indicates as "continuing." It seems as if all those elements interact with each other in his drawing, and that he can therefore balance them against each other—not as in a set of linear equations, but as in a set of hot-linked, nonlinear equations.

That the visual qualities are indeed essential to this process, and that the progression is not just the result of simply an improved verbal ability, is evident in the next example, in which the importance of visual qualities, such as color and texture is stressed. In this example, too, the verbal problem relates to Philippe's difficulty in dealing verbally with several factors simultaneously. The theme for this drawing was "hurricane," and it was done a couple of days after hurricane Gilbert struck the U.S. coast.

KDP: Do you know what a hurricane is? Have you heard about hurricane Gilbert?

Ph.: Yes. It is very dangerous.

KDP: Can you tell me why a hurricane is dangerous?

Ph.: Well, it is dangerous because of the very strong wind that hits the houses and everything.

KDP: Is that why people run away from it?

Ph.: Yes, they are afraid.

At this point, Philippe makes his drawing. (See figure 5.)

KDP: Now tell me about your drawing.

Ph.: Well, you see, you need to know the colors. They mean something. If you don't know the colors, you cannot understand the picture.

KDP: What do you mean? Can you show me what you mean? I think that the grey are clouds or rain, and that the green is grass, . . .

Ph.: Yes, that is easy. Everybody knows that . . . even you. (By that time he must have thought that I was really stupid, asking all

FIGURE 5.
Hurricane. Specific visual qualities such as color, texture and direction are used to convey a sense of simultaneity that Philippe cannot express verbally.

those questions.) Here (he points at the darker blue coming out of the house) I changed the color because in the house they have all this stuff.

KDP: What do you mean?

Ph.: Well, they maybe have like paint and other things that get in the water and change the color because of the dirt. And also you have rain (he points at the blue in the air) but also gray lines. That is the wind pushing at 120 miles per hour and the water from the sea (he points at the lighter blue) and the tiles from the roof (he now points at the black rectangles). And the rain seems as if the drops are connected because it is coming down so fast. That is why I made it like this (he points at the blue lines in the sky). And the branches are going in different directions because the wind is twisting. That is why I made the clouds go in two different directions. You see, the important thing is that everything happens at once.

KDP: What do you mean by that?

Ph.: I don't know. It is difficult to explain. (Silence). Do you know, I like to make those pictures. (Silence). You have neat markers.

In this example, even more than in the previous ones, different elements—rain, water, sea, clouds, dirt, etc.—feed back into each other, not in a linear sequence but simultaneously. "The important thing is that everything happens at once." What emerges is not a sequential story but the—necessarily linear—verbal translation of a multidimensional happening. Philippe, in a sense, is much more tuned in to the multidimensionality of the world around him. His problem with verbal language and its linear structure forces him, so to speak, to find other doors to the world. The drawings make it possible for him to get cognitively in touch with specific aspects of reality. The resulting perspective, however, is different from the one we get through a linear analysis; he has a better eye for the complex dynamics of his environment.

That his view is different does not mean that it is totally cut off from a "normal" perspective. The implication, rather, is that no particular perspective covers the entire range of possible cognition. Every perspective leaves particular gaps. Makeshift combinations of languages make it possible to leave fewer gaps in our overall view of the world. In Philippe's case, verbal language leaves huge blanks in his image of the world. The combination of verbal and visual language makes it possible for him to close some of the gaps, while at the same time it gives him access to some of the aspects of the world that would remain hidden from a strictly verbal perspective.

It is clear that in these examples, as well as in the ones that I present later in this book, a rich semantic structure was established, mediated by visual language. In a strictly verbal language, almost all cases of figurative language presented themselves to Philippe as unsolvable paradoxes, leading to either a complete denial of semantic content or to an arbitrary shifting around between incompatible semantic contents. In both cases, the reference of the figurative verbal language to the world had been lost, and this specific type of language, therefore, could no longer be meaningful. Philippe's understanding (if that term applies at all) of figurative verbal language is, in other words, the "understanding" of a Derridean text that consists of nothing but figurative language without reference to a world outside that language: such a text becomes either completely arbitrary or totally nonsensical.

The visual language that Philippe uses to bypass his verbal problem seems to resist paradoxicality, thereby allowing a richer, albeit perhaps a less precise, semantic structure. Since, of course, verbal and visual language, in their reference to the world and in their ontic structure, cannot be completely independent from one another, Philippe is able to "transpose"—at least partially—the visual semantic structure into a verbal semantic structure of which his explanations are the expression.

The major conclusion to draw here is that the reference of a word to the world is different from the reference of a visual or an auditory or a kinesthetic image to the world, and that the reference of discursive language is different from the reference of figurative language. That the verbal and the nonverbal, the discursive and the figurative, cannot be reduced to one another is probably the reason why in an evolutionary process a discursive verbal language might have had a surplus survival value. As all evidence seems to indicate, since our verbal abilities (e.g., the ability to speak) appeared long after our visual abilities (we could see before we could speak), there was visual language before verbal language. If such a discursive verbal language had merely been a different form of a basically identical way to organize the world, it would be very hard to understand why there would have been a need for such a verbal language, and more specifically why there would have been a need for discursive verbal language, which turns out to be the most precise, maybe, but also the least economical, of all possible combinations.

If the verbal and the nonverbal, the discursive and the figurative, are indeed to a large extent different ways of expressing knowledge and of knowing, and if the knowledge contained in each of them is not merely a redundant repetition of knowledge contained in one of the other forms (although some redundancy is certainly and necessarily the case), then a synthesis of the different forms of knowledge—verbal, visual, kinesthetic, and tactile, among others—

would maximize, or at least increase, the degree to which we are able to map our environment and react to it.

Interdisciplinary Language

I want to make a more specific point and claim that this synthesis of languages is a prerequisite, a necessary condition, for interdisciplinarity. I believe, in other words, that this is where the language of interdisciplinarity has to be found. Only in this pool of different ways of relating to the world will we be able to find sufficient referential and connective power to speak the language of which each of the disciplines is a level of complexity.

Introducing discursiveness or literality as a one-to-one relation and figurativeness as a many-to-many relation, it seems to me that a fundamental, but frequently made, mistake is the identification of denotation with discursiveness. Both discursive and figurative language can and do refer to the world, without reducing one to the other, without dealing with a many-to-many relation as nothing more than a complex form of a one-to-one relation. That discursiveness and figurativeness exist in a fundamentally symbiotic relation to each other—as do entropy and cybernetics, or disciplinarity and interdisciplinarity—does not mean that one of them can be crossed out and replaced by the other. While it can be argued that disciplinarity indeed requires discursiveness, to deal with the phenomena on each of the levels of reality that a specific discipline is concerned with, it can also be argued that interdisciplinarity requires a figurative language that can take our language beyond the boundaries imposed or required by the individual disciplines or languages. Interdisciplinarity, in other words, must claim the necessity of art and recognize the intrinsic, irreducible value of a language that can deal with the fundamental relation between structures, a fundamental relation beyond any specific or discursive comparison.

A synthesis or symbiosis of discursive as well as figurative visual, verbal, kinesthetic, and other forms of language will contribute to our ability to create inside our language a structure that is rich enough to refer to the structure of the world—a structure that goes beyond what we can create or recreate in discursive verbal language.

Some of the relations in, and properties of, the world are such that they can be more or less adequately dealt with in another language—human or not—only when that language is able to reach simultaneously different parts, different aspects, of the world it describes. Figurative language has that power. The very fact that art is highly valued in all societies suggests that there is a need for it that goes beyond the idea that it is just a sentimental souvenir, a once-maybe-useful but now completely out-of-date remainder from our evolutionary past. The world—our environment—is "suited" for figurative language because it is itself also figurative.

The exciting things that go on when children with an impaired ability to deal with verbal semantics combine verbal and visual language to develop rich semantic frameworks, illustrate the potential of such an approach. I believe that this approach fulfills the requirements for interdisciplinarity: Discursiveness and figurativeness are maintained simultaneously without losing the denotative aspect of either one, and without reducing either one to the other.

Chapter 4

Paradoxes and Self-Reference

Nothing in this book is true.
—*Kurt Vonnegut, Jr.*, Cat's Cradle

The Ontology of Semantic Paradoxes

Puns, metaphors, allegories, rhymes, and other figurative elements are important and powerful features of language. They push language to its limits, stretch its reach. Paradoxes, however, are different. Paradoxes threaten language in its very existence. They suggest that we can say whatever we might want to say and therefore that we can say nothing at all. In most logical systems, every single proposition that can be formulated, regardless of whether it is true or false, can be derived if the system contains a paradox. Starting from a series of seemingly perfectly acceptable and reasonable premises, a paradox leads to a conclusion that contradicts the foundation on which it was built. Paradox, to use William Poundstone's characterization, "is a travesty of the notion of proof."[1] Once a paradox has invaded the logical system—and they are very hard to keep out—the whole system looses credibility.

All paradoxes somehow imply the notion of contradiction. They can more or less be categorized according to when, where, and why the contradiction occurs. Fallacies, for example, are trivial mistakes, defective forms of argumentation. They include such things as the "proof" that 1 = 2, based on an implicit division by 0 (mathematical fallacy) and statements such as *All men can see, therefore a blind man can see,* a fallacy called "secundum quid," which is based on the deduction of a specific statement from a general statement without taking into consideration the specific conditions and restrictions related to the general statement. The contradiction expressed by the fallacy is only an illusion; it is sufficient to correct the mistake in the reasoning to get rid of the paradox.

In this work, I am dealing not with fallacies, but only with paradoxes caused by real contradictions—paradoxes that cannot be dealt with without substantially changing or affecting our understanding of the world. Moreover, I am concerned with paradoxes existing not only at the level of our human language, but also at the other levels of reality: physics, chemistry, biology, and so on. Such paradoxes, as I will try to show, had, and still have, the power to change the world; they were, and will continue to be, the driving force behind the increasing complexity of reality. Somewhat anticipating the more closely reasoned argument in this chapter, I propose that paradoxes can be solved only by the introduction of additional complexity. Complexity, in that sense, is the solution to paradoxicality menacing the very existence of the system in which it occurs. The distinct levels of reality that we acknowledge in our division of the world into successive layers really are levels of complexity added in order to solve paradoxes on the preceding levels.

Let us take a look at a well-known paradox that, according to Tarski, "tormented many ancient logicians and caused the premature death of at least one of them, Philetas of Cos":[2]

This sentence is false.

If the sentence is true, it is false; if it is false, it is true. This paradox is a version of the liar's paradox, generally attributed to the Greek philosopher Eubulides of the school of Megara. Another formulation of the same basic paradox comes from Epimenides the Cretan, saying, "All Cretans are liars."

In the liar's paradox it is not at all clear where a faulty premise or unacceptable reasoning might have caused the contradiction. Aristotle was one of the ancient philosophers to comment on the liar's paradox. In his work on logical fallacies, *De sophisticis elenchis,* he considered it to be similar to the perjurer's problem, which goes as follows: Does a man who swears to break his oath, break his oath when he breaks it? Aristotle's analysis dominated the work of classical and early medieval commentators. Later, however, Aristotle was proven wrong. The perjurer's paradox is merely an example of a fallacy; it is sufficient to understand that two different oaths are involved to solve the problem. Still other versions include the pseudomenon *I am now lying,* which is generally not used to analyze the paradox, because it involves aspects that are not intrinsic to the problem of the paradox—for example, a possible intent to deceive the listener.

There is also the mathematician Jourdain's card version of the paradox. Jourdain had cards printed that read on one side "The sentence on the other side of this card is TRUE" and on the other side "The sentence on the other side of this card is FALSE."[3] Jourdain's card version was actually an attempt to resolve the paradox by dividing the sentence of the *this sentence is false* version into two sentences that refer to each other. Karl Popper's version also consists of two statements, this time separated not in space, as in Jourdain's version, but in time: "The next assertion I am going to make is a true one" and "The last assertion I made was untrue." But, as Kainz points out, the problem with both Jourdain's and Popper's versions is that they transform the original paradox into the fallacy of vicious circularity, thereby eliminating the genuine self-reference that appears to be an essential ingredient of the liar paradox.[4] The self-reference, in other words, is pragmatically divided into two parts that can be considered to some extent independent from one another. The true liar paradox, however, is more than just a simple fallacy.

Where does the paradox in *This sentence is false* come from? It has been argued that the problem resides in the fact that the dichotomy "true-false" implies a bivalence—a two-valued logic that recognizes only black and white and nothing in between—that is too strong to be used and therefore leads to the paradox. However, it was later shown that rephrasing the paradox in terms of multiple-valued logics—a version referred to as the "strengthened" liar—does not eliminate the paradox.[5]

A multiple-valued system can, in many cases, adequately deal with the truth value of "ordinary" figurative language operating within a very complex and intricate syntactic, semantic, and pragmatic structure that allows for a multiple-valued, but not contradictory, meaning. A slip of the tongue, for example, might be attributed two separate truth values: one for the intended but unspoken sentence, and one for the unintended but spoken sentence. I do not want to get involved here in the debate concerning the intentionality of such mistakes. I only want to point out that such sentences, however confusing and ambivalent, are not paradoxes. It makes much more sense, I believe, to see these forms of figurative language as solutions to, for example, a mental or a social paradox: something we want to say but cannot. A slip of the tongue can be seen as a solution to a statement that has "This statement is false" written all over it. Figurative language attempts to overcome that paradox, that deadlocked situation, by incorporating both contradicting situations.

Figurative language, in that sense, acts as a local paradox-solving device: It clears the air, brings out the unspoken, and allows communication to continue on a new level of mutual understanding. The figurative allows for a certain distance from the original problem—in casu the paradox. This distance makes it possible to view both ends of the paradoxes as included in a single perspective, against a common horizon. The semantic jump in, for instance, a metaphor is consequently related to the jumps from one level of complexity of the world to another. The solutions to paradoxes in our language and the solutions to paradoxes in the world are structurally related. In terms of the everything-is-language hypothesis, they can all be qualified as involving figurative language.

Are paradoxes—the real ones, that is, not the fallacies—a problem that we should be concerned about? For most of us, in our everyday lives, they certainly are not. We do not come across real paradoxes that much, anyway, and even when we do, they never appear to be life-threatening. We can cope with them.

A number of philosophers have presented somewhat more sophisticated versions of this pragmatic perspective. They assert that paradoxes are a problem of logic and not of languages that are based in reality. Paradoxes arise only to the extent that our language does not refer to the world but deals with its own structure. A mathematical/logical foundation of a theory and the consequences that we can predict as a result are accepted to the extent to which the whole mathematical/logical structure, including the fundamental mathematics and the logical rules that are used to arrive at the predictions, remains consistent—free of paradoxes. That consistency (or, rather, coherency or the extent of that consistency, since most complex systems obviously cannot completely avoid paradoxes) combined with the almost uncanny accuracy of the numerical value of the predictions—what Eugene Wigner called "the empirical law of epistemology," the extent to which experiments and numerical predictions confirm each other—allows mathematics to become a part of theories in a very essential way, guiding us in our perspective, in looking at reality.

Concepts are expressed by mathematical symbols, and the symbols are given an interpretation in terms of the concepts. The behavior of particles, for example, is described in probabilistic terms, and probability has become an integral part of our concept of the world on the microscopic level. The result of such an interaction, to use Rohrlich's words, "is that the mathematical formulation of a theory contributes to the interpretation of the model of reality."[6] This process adds mathematics to our thinking as a dimension that goes beyond our everyday experience. In some cases (in quantum mechanics, for example), this leads to unexpected but exciting results, to interpretations of the mathematical structure of a theory that are hard to accept because they fundamentally change our understanding of the world. If such an interaction between theory and model includes paradoxes, so far, so good. We should not stop using logical systems because they occasionally generate paradoxes. That, at least, is the pragmatic attitude proposed by most authors attributing paradoxes to our human language and not to reality, eventually including our language.

A somewhat different version of this it-is-all-in-the-modeling approach is presented by J. D. Stone.[7] Stone, too, claims that we should not be concerned with the liar paradox: He rejects as being simplistic the dichotomy between true and not-true sentences that is implied by the paradox. Some relevant fact has not been taken into account, he contends. The question whether a sentence is true or not-true cannot be answered by a straightforward yes-or-no, and the distinction between true and false, which leads to the paradox, can therefore not be made correctly. As I have already indicated earlier in this chapter, making the system multiple-valued rather than binary does not solve the problem; ambiguity, vagueness, and context-dependence should be brought into the picture. Since these characteristics of natural language are, as Quine calls them, "mere nuisances" to the presentation of a formal (read: discursive) model of language, the semantic paradoxes such as the liar paradox set limits to the project of establishing a formal model of natural language. Semantic paradoxes, Stone concludes, are the result of an imperfect attempt to model natural language into a formal model. Human beings have a tendency to read the imperfections of the model back into the thing modeled, a tendency that may ultimately result in "a reductionist scheme in which the thing modelled is flatly identified with the model."[8]

I cannot but agree with Stone that "our taste for lean ontologies sometimes blinds us to the important disparities between model and thing modeled."[9] This was in fact my point about the tendency to identify interdisciplinarity with a reductionist search for an ultimate and unique formula. However, every language, and therefore also natural language, includes an attempt to model both itself and the objects outside itself. Even when Stone might not accept that an object outside the language in which it is described is itself always an element of another language—that, of course, is the implication of the everything-is-language hypothesis presented in this book—he should be able to accept my argument with respect to natural language itself (unless he were a Derridean, which he is not).

Natural language attempts to model the world. In doing so, it introduces a number of distinctions that may be more categorical than the actual distinctions on the level of the things modeled. "Red" and "green" cannot be identified on the level of physics without introducing an arbitrary distinction between two sets of wavelengths. Such a distinction is basically not different from the distinctions made within a formal model, which indeed may be more categorical than the distinctions made in natural language. Natural language, therefore, is as guilty of all the vices of modeling as any formal, logical model. Stone, from his point of view, contends that, "If English were a formal system, we would have to change to a different language to avoid contradiction"; I propose to replace this with "If English were a language (which it is), we would have to change to a different language to avoid the contradictions of English." And if that new language were a language (which it obviously is), we would have to . . . (etc.).

My point is that it is not just formal models of natural language that imply possible contradictions, but rather language in general. From my perspective, this includes all languages on all levels of reality. However, paradoxes, although structurally similar to each other, are language-specific. On the level of human language, this means that verbal and nonverbal, discursive and figurative, languages will behave differently with respect to paradoxicality. On the levels of the world outside our human language, it means that the level-specific languages—physics, chemistry, biology, and others—involve other paradoxes. The paradoxes of any one language are at least to some extent not the paradoxes of another language. That means that paradoxes in one language can be avoided or somehow bypassed by switching to another language. Such a makeshift of languages, I believe, is the driving force behind the increasing complexity of the world.

This point can be illustrated by confronting Stone's position with the one defended by Ronald Hepburn in *Christianity and Paradox*. While Stone describes paradoxes as arising from the failing attempts to cast natural language in a formal model that relies on binary oppositions, Hepburn defends the almost opposite view that paradoxes result from the stretching of natural language beyond its boundaries, beyond its limits. Rather than resulting from not taking into account ambiguity and vagueness, paradoxes are induced by an excess of ambiguity and vagueness. Words that are perfectly understandable in everyday contexts start to behave strangely when we use them in a very general and abstract way. Comparing the sentences *Outside my room a sparrow is chirping, Outside the city the speed limit ends, Outside the earth's atmosphere meteors do not burn out,* and finally *God is outside the universe, outside space and time,* Hepburn asks whether *outside* is not being stretched here to a breaking point, since *outside* gets its meaning precisely in the relation between objects or structures within space. The phrase *outside the universe,* Hepburn concludes, is "certainly still *grammatically,* though perhaps no longer logically, in order."[10] The theologian, of course, will counter this objection to his thinking by arguing that some mysteries can be talked about only in terms of paradoxes or not at all. Hepburn quotes Augustine as an example of such paradoxical language. To Augustine, God was "good without quality, great without quantity, a creator though he lack nothing, ruling but from no position, eternal yet not in time."[11]

Regardless of the attempts to establish contradictions as the result of a specific manipulation of language rather than of language in its "normal" use, and even though we can indeed usually get around paradoxes in our everyday use of language, the mainstream philosophical and scientific position is that paradoxes mean trouble. Whenever they occur in our attempts to understand the world, we know that something is wrong with our understanding and that we should proceed very cautiously.

Many philosophers therefore attempted to exclude or at least limit the self-reference of language that causes the paradoxes. They were never very successful, mainly because they failed—perhaps because paradoxes can be destructive—to integrate paradoxes as a meaningful, constructive element of the world. When they did away with paradoxes in a system, many of the interesting and constructive properties of the system had to be rejected also, resulting in a rather boring logical structure of little or no interest to our understanding of the world.

A number of these attempts to eliminate or reduce paradoxes are discussed further in this chapter. In the following pages, I will outline some elements of a theory of the world—an onto-epistemology—that not only includes paradoxicality, but considers paradoxes as one of its essential constituents, as the driving force, namely, behind the jump from ontology to epistemology.

I suggested earlier in this chapter that paradoxes are not unique to our human verbal language. Our paradoxes could be the equivalent on the human level of specific situations in the physical, chemical, biological, or cultural world. The basis for that contention, of course, is the idea that our language functions because its structure refers to the structure of the world outside our language. In order to address the implications of that hypothesis, two issues must be pursued: paradox in nonverbal language and paradox in the different languages of the world.

Paradoxes could be considered as the result of restrictions imposed on the relation between our language and the world. In that case, a paradox is neither "of the world" nor "of our human language," but rather belongs to the onto-epistemic relation between the world and ourselves. By extension, paradox belongs to the relation between any two levels that can be described in onto-epistemic terms. Whenever we cross the border defined by restrictions imposed on such a relation, a paradox follows.

In a verbal context, the sentence *God exists outside space and time* marks the breaking point where language was stretched beyond its literal reach and can continue to function only within a figurative context. Here, too, figurative language appears as a specific way of referring to the world, sufficiently different from a literal or discursive reference to avoid the paradoxicality that appears in the discursive context. As such, figurative verbal language manifests itself as a solution to a paradox in discursive verbal language. A shift in language—from a discursive toward a figurative language—would then be a way to get rid of the deadlocks we unavoidably encounter within any single language. What cannot be described scientifically could be described poetically. However, more drastic shifts could be considered: from a verbal to a nonverbal language, for example. When something cannot be said with words, it could be said with a drawing; when it cannot be drawn, we could try to paint, sing, or dance it.

I asked Philippe, who made the drawings in the second chapter, to help me out, in order to get a more precise idea of how verbal and visual language diverge as far as the tolerance on semantic stretching is concerned. We started with the same four sentences used by Hepburn to make a point about the limits of our verbal natural language: *Outside my room a sparrow is chirping, Outside the city the speed limit ends, Outside the earth's atmosphere meteors do not burn out,* and *God is outside the universe, outside space and time.* In this last sentence, Hepburn suggests, the meaning of *outside* is stretched beyond its breaking point. The sentences are especially interesting because, as a topological concept, *outside* has a clear visual reference. The relevant question at this point, of course, is whether in visual language we encounter the same breaking point as in verbal language.

Ph.: Does it have to be my exact room?
KDP: No.
Ph.: Can I go into details?
KDP: That is up to you.
Ph.: What color is that bird?
KDP: I have no idea.

Philippe finishes the first drawing, *Outside My Room a Sparrow Is Chirping,* and wants to explain it to me, but I ask him to finish the other drawings first to avoid an explicitly verbal interference with the next drawings. Working on the second drawing, *Outside the City the Speed Limit Ends,* he asks for a protractor "to make it perfect." Before starting on the third drawing, he asks me to read the sentence again.

KDP: Outside the earth's atmosphere, meteorites don't burn out.
Ph.: Do you want me to answer it?
KDP: It is not a question, it is a statement.
Ph.: Oh. I thought you wanted me to prove it.
KDP: Well, you can prove it if you want to.
Ph.: (after a while) I don't want to use words in this picture, but later I want to explain it to you.

Here too, as in his drawing about the hurricane described in the second chapter, we witness a major step forward in Philippe's attempts to use visual elements as parts of a cognitively meaningful and autonomous language. At this point in his development, visual language can be used to prove something, not just to imitate the visual qualities of our environment or to illustrate a verbal statement.

Before he starts working on the last drawing, Philippe tells me that I do not have to worry, he is not going to use up all my markers. He apparently has great plans. After he finishes the last drawing, he explains to me what he did in *Outside My Room a Bird Is Chirping.* (See figure 6.)

Ph.: Well, you have your room and you are listening. And you have a tree outside and you hear a bird whistling to you. OK?

FIGURE 6.
Outside My Room a Bird Is Chirping.

KDP: Why did you ask me whether it had to be your room?

Ph.: No, I was just . . . the setup of the room.

KDP: Is that important?

Ph.: No, I was just wondering. You said "outside my room," so I was just wondering.

KDP: Does it make a difference as far as the sentence is concerned?

Ph.: No. It does in a way, because some rooms might not have a window.

KDP: What would that mean?

Ph.: That would mean that they would not hear the bird, because there would be walls and they couldn't hear it through the walls.

KDP: But the bird would still be outside?

Ph.: Yes.

Then we move on to the second drawing, *Outside the City, the Speed Limit Ends.* (see figure 7.)

Ph.: You see, I wanted to make a city, because you know how all cities are so perfect and all buildings are so perfect. I wanted to make one that you wouldn't recognize or anything. And once you leave that area, that highly place of authority, you can't go anymore, you just stop. You have to turn back because the speed limit ends and it is sort of like automatically that your car turns off and won't go.

KDP: You mean that the engine is turned off?

Ph.: Yes, the whole car stops. So you have . . . it forces you, it is pointing you to come back to the city, so nobody will leave. So there is somebody who rules it who is keeping all the people in the city. So when you try to walk out of the city you are pulled back, there is no speed limit anymore. And you go back to your normal life but there is this one guy who is ruling it all.

KDP: Is this "outside the city" a different "outside" than the one in "outside your room"?

Ph.: Oh, yes. You have your room and you have your downtown and then there is outside. But this one (outside the city) is different because it is pulling you back and that outside (outside your room) is going away.

While explaining his drawing to me, Philippe was actually, and apparently very consciously, trying to construct a verbal figurative

FIGURE 7.
Outside the City, the Speed Limit Ends.

expression *Outside the city the speed limit ends.* Later he told me that he knew that the speed limit did not end outside the city, that you can go faster but that there is still a speed limit. So, instead of concluding that it was a false statement—as he would have done at an earlier stage of his dealing with verbal language—Philippe decided to do something with it. Admittedly, the result is not the winner of the

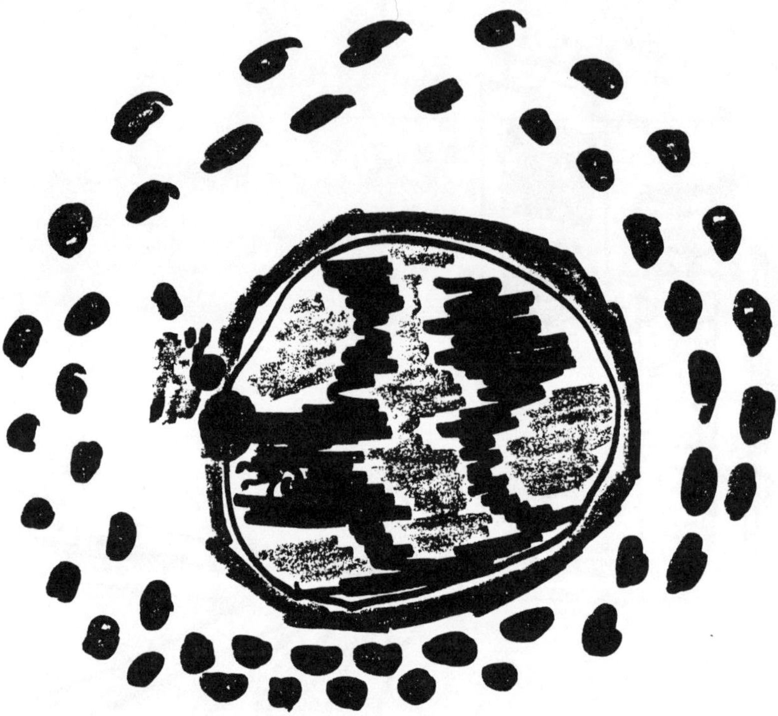

FIGURE 8.
Outside the Earth's Atmosphere, Meteorites Don't Burn Out.

Figurative Language Award. His verbal explanation is rather clumsy and inefficient, but the process nevertheless induced a complex understanding of "outside." As a matter of fact, it appears as if, as far as Philippe is concerned, the discursive verbal language already reached its breaking point—much earlier than most speakers would admit it does within a strictly verbal frame. This observation is confirmed by the way in which Philippe deals with the third drawing, *Outside the Earth's Atmosphere, Meteorites Don't Burn Out.* (see figure 8.)

Ph.: This skeleton—the pink thing—is the ozone layer which protects us. When it (he points at one of the brown dots) comes down it starts burning and then it's hot when it is on fire and then when it gets down there it's gone, it's finished. But there are some that make it, but they will always burn.

KDP: So some meteorites may eventually hit the ground?

Ph.: Yes.

KDP: What is the meaning of "outside" here?

Ph.: It means that you are safe outside and the inside is scary.

KDP: You are safe outside?

Ph.: Yes.

KDP: Who is safe outside?

Ph.: The meteorites. They are safe from the world, but that would be like in many examples. When you have a State National Park, and say you have is three-fourths of the United States, and then that one-fourth is right in the middle, then the people—all the animals in the national wildlife park are protected from that inside. And they're protected so nobody can go out there and shoot them because if they do they get penalized—do you know what I mean? And so that's like when an animal is stupid enough to go into the city, it is probably gonna die. And that's like if the meteorite goes into the world, it is gonna die.

Philippe obviously continued to build on what he started in the first two drawings: a complex, multidimensional mapping of the concept of "outside" onto different structures: social order, cosmological orders, and so on. That may sound like not very much, but what emerges here is a much more complex semantic pattern than most people would come up with based on just the verbal sentences. Philippe, of course, does not abide by the literal meaning of each of the sentences, but that is exactly the point: The overlapping between verbal and visual language allows him to make a semantic shift that, while consistent with the verbal framework, goes way beyond it in its connective power.

We move on to the final drawing. (See figure 9.)

Ph.: We have the world, and then you have . . . you have earth, and then you have the universe, and then you have all the stars that are way far away. And those (he points at the openings in the black "cloud" over the earth) are little cracks in the heaven.

KDP: Is not everything in the universe?

Ph.: Yes, I know, and all these little stars are like the farthest point away. And then there's the little cracks in heaven. But then . . .

FIGURE 9.
God Is Outside the Universe, Outside Space and Time.

KDP: Where is heaven?

Ph.: It is beyond everything.

KDP: When you are beyond everything, could you still say that you are in space?

Ph.: No.

KDP: Where does it end?

Ph.: It ends right near the little stars, at the very end. It ends, you can't go farther.

KDP: Why can't you go any farther? Remember how you can always count further, how you can always add one more number . . . it never ends.

Ph.: Yes, but it is impossible, it doesn't work. It is like when you try to divide 1 . . . 10 into 0, it doesn't work. (Silence).

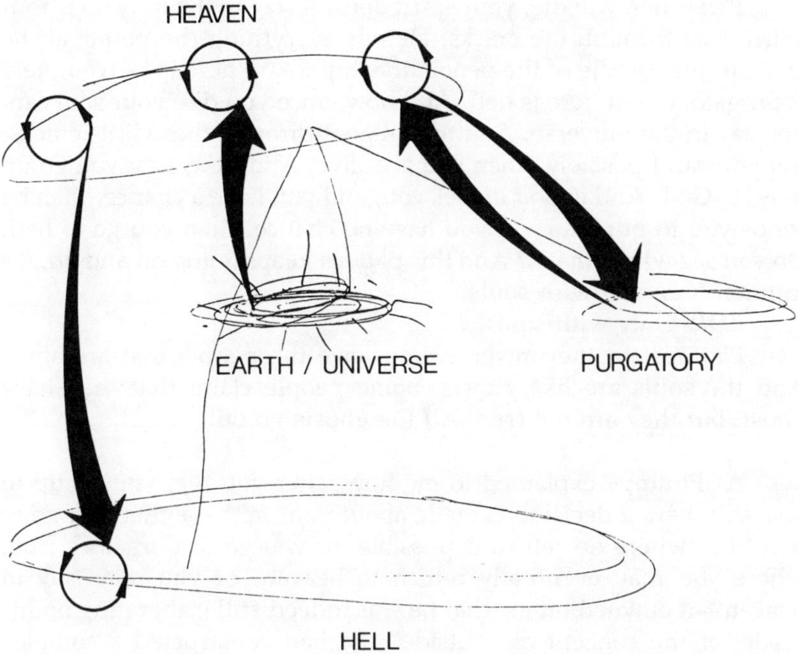

FIGURE 10.
Earth, Heaven, Hell, and Purgatory. The added arrows formally indicate the different accessibility relations that Philippe has included in his drawing.

KDP: Is that what is going on here?

Ph.: Yes, it doesn't work. You can't get outside. But then when you are outside, when you get past that space, then you have spirits of people that are not in the universe and you have God.

I kept telling him that I didn't understand what he was trying to explain. At that point, Philippe took a new piece of paper and, using only pencil, made a quick sketch of what turned out to be earth, heaven, hell, and purgatory. As he had just been transferred to a Catholic school a few months earlier, I assume that is where he got the vocabulary from; never before his recent transfer did he get any formal or consistent instruction in religion.

Ph.: When you die, your spirit doesn't stay in the universe. Your spirit goes through the cracks. Here is everything (he points at the circle in the middle of the pencil drawing). And here is heaven, here is purgatory, and here is hell. And now, once you die, your soul cannot stay in the universe. And then it goes through those little cracks. But you can't possibly when you are alive. And now, first you go up here, to God. And if God denies you, and you have a chance, then he sends you to purgatory. If you have no chance, then you go to hell. Do you see what I mean? And this pattern keeps going on and on, it's infinite. It is only with souls.

KDP: Only with souls?

Ph.: Yes. In the universe, you have the people that are alive. And the souls are like ghosts. Some people claim that they have ghost, but they are not true. All the ghosts go out.

As Philippe explained to me how, after you die, you go up to heaven where a decision is made about your faith—either you go to hell from where no return is possible, or you go to purgatory from where you may eventually return to heaven, or you may stay in heaven—it dawned on me that he was indeed still elaborating on his model of the concept of "outside"; he had constructed a complex model of accessibility relations and conditions imposed on these relations.

Comparing what transpires in verbal language with visual language—in casu Philippe's drawings—it was obvious that visual language did not reach a sudden breaking point as did verbal language. Visual language, rather, shifted earlier and more gradually toward a figurative interpretation. It is therefore reasonable to assume that paradoxes, in such a nonverbal context, will not take the same form as they do in verbal language. It is even reasonable to claim that in several cases where we would encounter a verbal paradox, we will not find a visual or any other nonverbal paradox.

These findings raise several questions about the nature of paradoxes. Is a sudden and unexpected appearance, for example, essential to paradox, or not? Is the sudden appearance only specific to verbal paradoxes? Can a statement be "barely," "50 percent," or "almost" paradoxical? These and other questions are important, because they have significant implications for the ontological status of paradox. Earlier, I indicated self-reference as being essential to paradox, of which the statement *This sentence is false* was a clear example. Now we must ask if we can find a meaning of "truth" that an image can apply to itself. Can an image—a painting, for example—call itself false? If so, what does *false* mean then?

To understand paradox as an essential constitutive element in all possible languages, we must understand how reflexivity is operative in all of them. A tentative answer to that question, with regard to visual language, might be that images—whether or not literally representational—are reflexive to the extent that they have become what they deal with, to the extent that they have emulated or assimilated some of the basic structures of the world they refer to, and to the extent that they always exist in the world. To the extent that a language has become what it deals with, and to the extent that a language always exists in the world that it refers to, language cannot but also deal with itself. In the next chapter, in relation to this issue of assimilation, I will discuss the epigenetic development of neurological structures that "become like the world" they relate to through sensory impressions. I propose that a similar point can be made about language in general, not just about the language of neural networks. Language, I believe, assumes some of the basic patterns and structures it refers to. As a result, operations on elements within a language system appear as similar, although very likely not as identical, to operations on elements in the world outside the specific language. Even so apparently completely arbitrary a system as a binary computer language cannot escape this phenomenon, if only in the basic fact that the language can function only if one can make a distinction between 1 and 0 and that it can no longer be meaningful if a specific memory location were to be both 1 and 0—a paradox.

To the extent that truth is an expression of reference to the world, and to the extent that language, any language, can exist only in the world, truth will always imply self-reference. The consistency between what language claims about the world and what it claims about itself then appears as a crucial test of truth. That is why paradoxes of the liar type are so important: They mark cases where the consistency between world and language seems irretrievably gone, thereby threatening the ability of language to say anything truthful about the world at all.

All language, including visual language, can in principle be reflexive and can therefore express semantic paradoxes. A general statement like this, of course, does not tell us how and under what conditions semantic paradoxes will appear in a specific language. Consistent with the idea that paradoxes are crucial to interdisciplinarity and the idea that interdisciplinarity can never be a quest for a single reductionist formula, paradoxes too will need to be specified for each of the constituting languages of the world.

Levels of Reference

One of the most elegant ways to handle paradoxes of the liar type is to introduce the concepts of object language and metalanguage. The basic idea behind that approach is fairly simple and mainly based on Tarski's analysis of semantic paradoxes. To replace *this sentence* by *"this sentence"* (*this sentence* in quotes) is to eliminate the self-reference on the level of *this sentence* and to replace it by a reference made from the level of the quotation marks.

In other words, in order to maintain consistency, the partial reflexivity of language—partial because we do not have to go to another level, and because total reflexivity on a single level implies a closed system—has forced us to create two distinct levels of reference. The two levels, although intimately related, cannot be reduced to one another, since then the paradox would be reinstated. Although self-reference can still occur on each of the individual levels, an escape route has been put in place.

The reason why, in a nutshell, these levels of complexity are so important is because they turn the self-reference of language into a constructive, rather than a destructive, tool or quality. On the newly created level a new structure can be developed, although restricted by the conditions imposed by its origins. The combination of reflexivity and consistency has generative power!

We need to establish that this generative system will continue to generate new levels of complexity. In other words, we need to show either that paradoxes cannot be solved permanently or that the solution to a paradox will, in principle, lead to new paradoxes.

Some paradoxes indeed express or indicate that we cannot reach a level where complete reflexivity and complete consistency can be realized simultaneously—for example, Cantor's set-theoretical paradox, which refers to "the set of all sets that do not contain themselves as an element." If that set—let's call it A—does not contain itself, it should be an element of A, but A would then contain itself, so that A would no longer contain only sets that do not contain themselves as an element. Bertrand Russell offered a somewhat more accessible formulation of this paradox. In a certain village the barber shaves *all* the men who do not shave themselves, and he shaves *only* those. The pertinent question then is, Who shaves the barber? If he does not shave himself, then he must be shaved by—the barber. But since he is the barber, the barber would shave himself and would therefore no longer shave only those men who do not shave themselves.

These paradoxes necessitate the creation of more and more levels of complexity in order to take care of the inconsistencies that arise on every new level that is generated to resolve the inconsistencies of the previous level. In other words, once a new level is introduced to cope with a paradox on the previous level, the problem of the liar paradox is not really solved once and for all: The problem potentially repeats itself on the newly created level. *This sentence is false* leads to *'This sentence' is false,* but on that new level, we might say *'This sentence' is false. This sentence is false.* We have to make it clear that this means *" 'This sentence' is false" is false*—whereby, once again, a new level of complexity is introduced, for to make that distinction we must look at the paradox from a distance, created when we look at the problem from a higher level.

The next constitutive element needed to establish a working generative system that we can use to understand the totality of the world rather than just our human language is expressed in Gödel's theorem, which states that consistent systems contain true statements that cannot be proven by the system. The interaction between Gödel's theorem—the argumentation of which is quite technical and can be omitted for simplicity's sake—and liar-type paradoxicality is "responsible" for the relative uniqueness and independence of each of the levels of reality. When a system creates a next-higher level to regain the consistency that it lost when one of its levels ran into semantic paradoxes, then from Gödel's work it follows that the newly created next-higher level will contain a true sentence that cannot be derived from the lower levels. Biology is more than just chemistry. It contains a true expression, "life," that cannot be reduced to the level of chemistry. As a result, the levels of reality cannot be reduced to one another without losing the consistency gained when new levels of complexity are introduced. If it were at all possible to specify a unique formula from which all the others could be generated or derived without adding something new, then such a formula would necessarily contain or lead to paradoxes. These paradoxes, then, could in principle not be avoided, because solving paradoxes is possible only by introducing novelty, by creating new levels of reality that in turn will necessitate further levels of complexity.

That conclusion may have considerable implications for any interdisciplinary theory. First of all, it provides a firm foundation for my claim that individual disciplines cannot be replaced by an interdisciplinary theory: Only individual disciplines can deal with the novelty that is created on each of the levels of complexity. Furthermore, if we accept the premises that I presented earlier, we also have to accept that an interdisciplinary theory will contain true sentences or propositions that cannot be derived from the totality of the specific sciences or disciplines on which the interdisciplinary theory is founded. Any interdisciplinary theory will have to make claims that are true but that cannot be shown to follow from our level-specific knowledge. On the other hand, it also follows that it is impossible to just assume that higher levels will completely include lower levels so that we might as well do away with those now-no-longer-useful levels. *'This sentence' is false* has no meaning whatsoever if the level of *this sentence* is done away with. At its best, *'This sentence' is false* would then read *This sentence is false*—which would reinstate the paradox. Paradoxes, in that case, would be purely destructive. Our own existence proves that they are not.

Although for all practical purposes a sufficiently rich language can function without a constant danger of inconsistency caused by self-reference, it is the *limits* of the language at any given level—limits reached when a level runs into fundamental paradoxes—that are the *creative force* behind its expansion into higher, more complex levels. "Sufficiently rich" is a crucial term here that we can at this point not further define. If the language were not sufficiently rich, if, as a matter of fact, it were so poor that it would lack expressions to describe the basic properties of the world in which it exists, the problem of self-reference might be avoided altogether. Not so, however, if the world *itself* were language; in that case any language would be rich enough to allow for self-reference if at least its output were persistent enough to be available as input for, or as an element of, the language. Self-reference, in other words, cannot be avoided in a world of language that has a minimal form of memory—that is, an order maintained in time, an ontology.

Internally Open Systems

In this context, one approach to paradoxicality—its relation with semantically closed systems—should be given special consideration. In this section, I will attempt to indicate why a prototypical and influential version of that approach—Hegel's dialectical idealism—fails and how it is related to Derrida's equally inadequate position.

Hegel's *Phänomenologie des Geistes* can be read as an attempt to establish a path on which propositions or syllogisms follow from each other according to an internal necessity, leading to the teleological end of both organic and inorganic nature—to the Absolute Idea. Methodologically, in his writing as well as with regard to the subject matter of his work, everything is determined and already present at the very origin of the *Phänomenologie des Geistes* as a philosophical investigation and the *Phänomenologie des Geistes* as the subject of that investigation. The semantic closure becomes evident at the end of history but is *an sich* present from the beginning of history.

Hegel describes how the "neutral product," which is the result of the reaction between an acid and a base, supersedes and cancels the original distinction, which was therefore not a "real" distinction in the first place, but merely a distinction between predicates, which, in the reaction between the subjects to which they were attached, are freed from their subjects and are found to be universal.[12] It is my understanding that at this point (or at any other point where Hegel makes a similar argument) the semantic closure is established. In the process of the reaction between base and acid, the world becomes a little bit more flat, stripped of one more level of detail. The opposition—*contradiction* being too strong a term here—between base and acid has been made meaningless, without reference.

Solving a paradox, in Hegel's semantically closed universe as well as in Derrida's semantically closed text, results in an increase of entropy. Such a closed system can be internally dynamic, maybe, but only in an irreversibly destructive way, leading to a state of maximal and permanent equilibrium.

In a closed system such as Hegel's or Derrida's, the existence of true sentences that do not follow from the theory can be avoided, thereby making Gödel's theorem irrelevant. A closed system, namely, will accept only those sentences, if any, that can be dealt with from within the system—for example, the material implication in classical logic. But Gödel's theorem states that this system will be either incomplete (some true sentences will not be recognized as such) or inconsistent (recognizing all the true sentences without assuming a new level of description will make the system inconsistent).

Truth can be complete and consistent only in a system in which some true sentences are recognized as such from a higher level of description, a level on which new true sentences will exist that in turn cannot be described completely and consistently without introducing a next level of description. Those new true sentences, I have argued, are the ones that assure that language will never close completely upon itself. To establish the truth of those Gödelian sentences, we need to assume a relation that goes beyond the system in which a proof is formulated. That is exactly where the threatening closure, at that point already leading to inconsistency, is avoided. We cannot, in other words, recognize the paradoxes as such in a completely closed system. A good example is classical logic, where every true proposition entails nothing but itself and other true propositions—simply because in such a system true and false can no longer be distinguished from each other. Semantic closure, therefore, necessarily turns language into a flat object. Innovation and creation are no longer real options. We appear to be creative, but in reality we are not; the only possible changes are those that rigorously follow the path that maintains the semantic closure.

The level on which the law of noncontradiction could be formulated is *not* the level of the contradictory sentences or propositions, even if both the sentences *and* the law were expressed in the same language, say Swedish, Italian, or a classical logic, which does not allow p & $-p$ based on the law of noncontradiction $-(p$ & $-p)$, expressed on a metalevel within its language. We need a higher level to express that noncontradiction should be a law or a general principle. The very existence of a higher level of complexity is itself the expression of the principle of noncontradiction.

It is necessary to show that semantic paradoxicality can and does have the generative function that I have discussed earlier. We are again confronted with the basic question, Why can we say things that are wrong if we want to say things that are right? This time, the questions takes on a somewhat different form: Why is language inconsistent if we want it to be consistent? That language is inconsistent because of self-reference is no more than a partial answer. Leaning toward a mild, generalized form of the anthropic principle, we could argue that language is reflexive and therefore inconsistent because it allows language to be what I would like to call *an internally open*—and hence figurative—*system*, a system capable of internal expansion and differentiation without external leverage, a system that can exist without, as I will argue in chapter 6, having to postulate an absolute origin beyond space and time, without having to assume that it is contingent upon the existence of an absolute being, that is, God.

A sufficiently rich language or system of languages, such as our human language, can in principle refer to any given level of complexity, since its internal open-endedness will make it possible to construct that same complexity within its own structure. Again, while it seems as if our language never escapes its inherent limits—which I believe is true—this turns out to be one of our language's most powerful and constructive aspects. It means that we are in principle able to stretch the reality of our language way beyond the complexity of our physical, chemical, biological, and even cultural environments.

The Reference of Visual Self-Reference

That language allows us to stretch reality—and that, I believe, is one of the major characteristics and functions of art—acutely puts forward the question of the reference of language in general and the self-reference of language in particular. The self-reference of our understanding—in other words, the reflexivity of our knowledge—quite literally adds language to the world and, therefore, adds to the world. The internally open and hence figurative structure of our language and of the world outside our language, capable of internal expansion and differentiation without external leverage, gives us every reason to assume that the self-reference of our understanding is a potential source of paradoxicality and therefore of a continued change and growth of the world.

The paradoxes caused by the reflexivity of our understanding are, as I argued earlier, language-specific. As the reference of verbal language to the world is different from the reference of nonverbal language to the world, reflexivity of verbal language will necessarily be different from reflexivity of nonverbal language. Consequently, the paradoxes of verbal language cannot be the paradoxes of nonverbal language.

Several volumes could be filled with references to publications on verbal self-reference. This is not the place to elaborate on the merits of each of the different approaches presented thus far. However, I would like to include two additional examples of Philippe's work—two drawings that specifically deal with the problem of visual self-reference.

I was curious to find out how far Philippe would be able to take his newly found visual methodology. So we moved on to something more serious: Kant's use of the notion of "horizon" to deal with the conditions and properties of knowledge. "Horizon," obviously, is a visual concept used in a figurative sense in verbal language. The question was how Philippe, given his tremendous difficulties with adequately understanding figurative verbal language, would do when dealing visually with this figurative language and the visual self-reference it implies.

KDP: Do you know what the horizon is?

Ph.: Yes, it is where the sun is going down. It is as far as you can see.

KDP: The horizon of knowledge—does that mean anything to you?

Ph.: It is as far as knowledge goes.

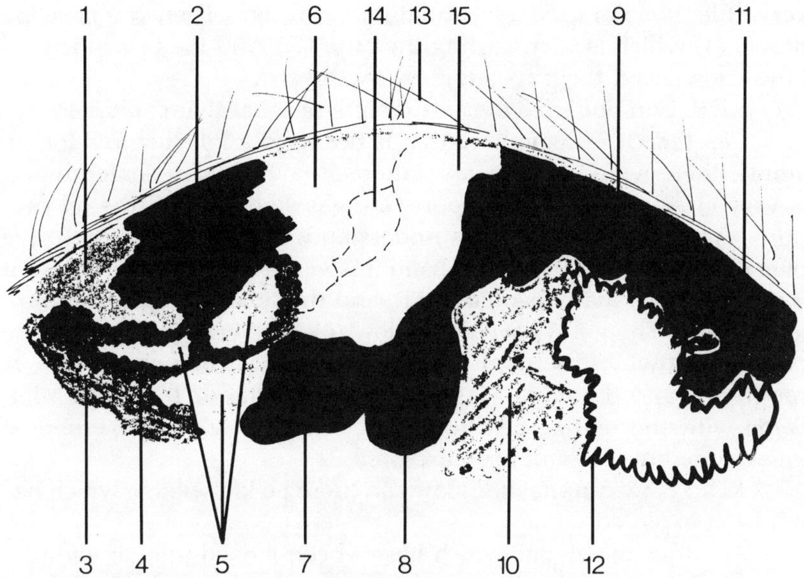

FIGURE 11.
The Horizon of Knowledge. The numbers refer to the text.

After this brief conversation, Philippe starts working on his drawing. (See figure 11.) The following is the transcription of his explanation after he finished it. As usual, his verbal account is not exactly easy to follow, but it gives a fairly good idea of the power of his visual thinking.

Ph.: In some places there is knowledge, but it hasn't been explored. I'll explain everything to you. This one (the red on the left [1]), it has a little rough edge, it's smooth along the border which . . . all of them are going to be smooth along the border, but they might have a different meaning. OK? It has rough spots because the blue next to it (2) has blended in rough. But this one is smooth and understood well. So it's very common. It's used a lot, you see?

KDP: What is smooth? The red one?

Ph.: The red one . . . that type of knowledge. Say, mathematics, that is. It is for example, you see. And that's used a lot. Now the green one (the light green on the left [3]), it is very rough. And it is very little, it is not used a lot and it is very rough. Then you have the brown (4) which is surrounding the pink (5). And the brown is very little known and the pink supports the brown.

KDP: Can you give me an example of what that could be?

Ph.: OK. It is something that is not used a lot. Just say, for example, there weren't many gas stations. Maybe two or something. It is very little and the gas supports the gas station. And the oil supports the gas station. Do you understand? And then you have the blue (2) right next to the red (1) and it is very rough but big. So what it means is that many people use it, and that many people don't understand it. Then you have the yellow (6). It is very smooth but the only reason why it is rough is because it is next to a rough one. A rough one and the white (14). Do you understand? It is used a lot. Same with the orange next to it (15). And the white (14), there is knowledge but it hasn't been explored.

KDP: How can that be? How can there be knowledge which has not been explored?

Ph.: It is knowledge which hasn't been looked into far enough, but people know about it. And then you have the black (7) under it which is very smooth and it has been used a lot. Then you have the purple (8) which is only used as one area but it is used just like in a certain formation, do you know what I mean? Like our telephones here, they work on this net. It is like it works on one huge satellite or something, so it only works in that area. OK? And then you have the green (9) which is smooth and it is like maybe cars that are used a lot.

KDP: Cars? What have cars to do with knowledge?

Ph.: Well, I am just giving examples. No, OK, maybe computers. Tools. And then you have the grey (10). It is been researched but it is very sketchy and they can research it much more. Like say the moon, it is been researched. Or no, say Mars. We know it is there but we haven't researched it enough. And then you have the light blue (11) which is been researched a lot. Then you have the red (12) which is a very sketchy one, which is just a little bit of it, just the outer layer of it. It has been researched and the rest hasn't.

KDP: So this map is a map of the things about which we have knowledge? What has "horizon" to do with that?

Ph.: That is just where it stops and then there is no more. It is nothing.

KDP : What is beyond there? Why did you make the grey marks (13) above the horizon?

Ph.: Well, maybe it goes a little farther. But people think there is knowledge but there is none.

KDP: But there is nothing to see?

Ph.: No. There is nothing to see. Like you dig for gold in a building where you know there is not going to be gold, you know?

In the heat of our conversation, I decide to push Philippe somewhat on this subject.

KDP: People used to think that the earth was a flat circle and that the horizon actually was the end of the world, something they would fall off if they came too close.

Ph.: Yes, I know that.

KDP: But aren't you doing something like that? When you move, your horizon moves with you.

Ph.: But this time, there is nothing really behind it. Nothing. Do you understand? It is like what they used to think, but, say, they were correct.

KDP: But aren't there things that you didn't know before, and now you do? Or things we don't know about yet, but maybe we will be able to understand in the future?

Ph.: Yes. Of course. But, you see, that is all in the colors, when you move from one color to another and you find out new things.

Philippe, who most of the time resists any figurative interpretation of verbal language, has actually created a visual reference frame—a fractal image, in some sense—in which he can simultaneously deal with figurative verbal language, paradoxes, interference from different fields of knowledge, accessibility from one field to another, and so on. Even stronger: He now resists the literal, reductive interpretation that I suggested to him when I pointed out how people mistakenly used to think that the earth was a flat object.

I asked him to make one more drawing. "Perspective" is a concept used to specify our view on the world. As such, it is a metaconcept that expresses some of the qualities of visual perception. The new drawing was about "perspective on knowledge"—taking the reflexive levels of visual language one step further. (See figure 12.)

Ph.: When you look at knowledge, you have your big circle of knowledge and so you can have little slices in the sides of it. And

FIGURE 12.
Perspective on Knowledge.

that's the way you are looking at it. And then you might have knowledge looked at by a left person—and so he uses his right brain, which is more creative, and so he might come at it this way. But you might have a right-handed person who might come at it this way. And then you might have persons who can use both their hands, you know, and they might come in this way.

KDP: . . .

Ph.: And then you might have people who can talk many different languages, and they might come this way. Do you understand? Just looking at it, it looks foreign from there on. And there may be advantages to it, because the person that uses his right brain is very creative, right, and might see things like that. Like a blind person, especially a left-handed blind person, he can feel everything and know what is, you know.

KDP: Who told you that?

Ph.: I know that. Well, there was this show, once. And then I learned from myself that if you are blind you use your feel a lot. They might come in and learn many secrets. But then sometimes there are other things they cannot get. Like when I do nouns, and definitions, I couldn't get it. But then in math, I pick up the system like that. And then there are other things that I need to go over and over and then finally it snaps. And then these drawings, that is like a perspective of how I see things. Like, you make a drawing of the horizon of knowledge, you might have words on it, and words and words, and formulas. You might have used different colors, little things.

KDP: And that would have made a difference?

Ph.: Well, maybe you would have thought that the rough parts have been explored already, so you would have changed that, made it smooth. You may have seen things different, which you probably do, and your wife might see it different than you, but then there are people who might see it exactly the same. Like in class, I was just thinking about that, the teacher said something and the student next to me said, "I was just thinking that." They both thought of the same thing. Do you understand?

Philippe, of course, is a very bright boy, but it is nevertheless remarkable how visual language allows an eleven-year-old child to reflect upon subjects that most adults would not comfortably discuss. It should be clear that visual language is an extremely versatile and powerful tool, even for people who do not produce an artistic masterpiece every time they pick up a pencil. But, then, how many of us ever qualified for the Nobel Prize for literature?

It is essential, I believe, that we are not confined to a single solution to a problem. Quite often, a range of possible solutions is available to us, even though we tend to single out one solution as "better" than the others. Verbal language, for example, has been singled out as "the better cognitive tool." Nevertheless, it becomes increasingly clear that nonverbal languages are also essential to our understanding of the world. In some cases, as in Philippe's, such an alternative solution may even emerge as the preferred solution. In the next chapter, then, we will focus mainly on the evolutionary aspects of the emergence of solutions.

Chapter 5

Performing the Language of Evolution

If man is a sapient animal, a toolmaking animal,
a self-making animal, a symbol-using animal,
he is, no less, a performing animal, Homo performans,
not in the sense, perhaps, that a circus animal
may be a performing animal, but in the sense
that man is a self-performing animal—his performances
are, in a way, reflexive, *in performing he reveals*
himself.
—*Victor Turner,* The Anthropology of Performance.

Evolution as Reflexive Language

We cannot but notice some of the fascinating connections between the generative system that I have outlined in the previous chapters and biological evolution; connections existing between consistency and survival, between entropy and variation or mutation, and between heredity and cybernetics.

In certain cases, those connections are quite obvious. Our own human language is literally based on a very gradual evolutionary process on the biological level. In *The Biology and Evolution of Language,* Philippe Lieberman describes how human language evolves as the result of positive feedback from a cultural environment into the biological. Human-like creatures—which were already using their hands to manipulate tools and carry objects, the result of previous sequences of anatomical changes such as the development of the opposable thumb and the changes that made an upright bipedal locomotion possible—developed the ability to produce a wider range of distinct features that in turn facilitated the development of speech. "The evolution of human linguistic and cognitive ability," as Lieberman puts it, "thus is part of the general process of human evolution."[1]

It goes almost without saying that such an evolution is not a linear path proceeding from a genesis in a distant past to a fulfillment somewhere in the future. At almost every stage of the evolutionary process, differentiation is an essential element. Jay Dowling and Dane Harwood, in *Music Cognition,* propose that cultural variability of musical behavior is constrained—and is therefore, as I have argued before, also made possible—by some of the underlying properties of the human information-processing system. This, of course, includes the developments described by Lieberman, but also even more fundamental mathematical and physical properties of sound waves. Dowling and Harwood specifically refer to such universals as the use of discrete pitch intervals, octave equivalence, and the presence of four to seven focal pitches in an octave.[2] What seems particularly interesting in their work is the suggestion that these universal constraints on lower levels—for example, the ability to make a distinction between consonance and dissonance—are to some extent put to different uses in different cultures. In other words, constraints or limits on, for instance, the anatomical or neurological level literally open up a range of perspectives on the next level. In chapter 6, I will specify that range of perspectives as a range of possible events, each with its own probability.

An interpretation of the generative, internally open system introduced in the previous chapter as being a minimal model for language in general (i.e., not just a model for human language or verbal language) brings us excitingly close to the understanding that *language is evolution,* or, for that matter, that *evolution is language:* a continuous search for solutions, adaptations, connections, the use of previously established patterns in new and more complex situations, and so on. We even catch a glimpse of how our human language, with its simultaneous existence on and reference to several distinct levels of complexity (quantum physics, chemistry, biology, etc.), could be the interdisciplinary language par excellence. Simultaneity is exactly what figurative language can accomplish and what it is all about. Poetic language, therefore, in the sense of both verbal and nonverbal figurative language, is crucial to interdisciplinarity: It provides us with simultaneous access to several distinct levels of reality.

This also means that figurative language—such as poetry—is not just a cultural phenomenon. Rather than being a culturally biased and therefore contingent expression of our most personal feelings, it is the language that connects us with all the levels of the rich structure in which we exist. As such, the language connecting a nonhuman level of reality to any of the other levels will equally be figurative language. In other words, figurative language is not an exclusively human feature.

The idea that evolution—as a factual process in the world and not as a specific theory of how evolution works—is not limited to biological systems has been widely accepted and promoted. Hahlweg and Hooker, for instance, attempt to establish an evolutionary model that is expressed as the evolution of complex regulatory systems. Such systems, they contend, can be found not only in the genotypic and phenotypic organization of biological systems, but also in scientific concepts, methods, theories, and so forth. They understand scientific evolution, therefore, as "a literal extension of biological evolution."[3] Nevertheless, however interesting this approach may be, I fail to understand why the functioning of evolutionary processes in prebiological systems is seldom acknowledged. Evolution, if one is to go along with the implicit suggestions in almost all of the literature on the subject, came into being with biology.

In *The Tree of Knowledge: The Biological Roots of Human Understanding,* Maturana and Varela use the aphorism "All doing is knowing, and all knowing is doing"[4] as the bottom line of their research. They explicitly limit the "doing"—which they identify as dealing with language—to the domain of biology. Only living things can know. As they see it, the roots of knowledge go all the way back to the level of biology—but not beyond. Their criterion for making that claim is organization, defined as the relations that must exist among the components of a system if they are to belong to a specific class. Biological organisms, in particular, are characterized by what Maturana and Varela call their "autopoietic organization," of which the most striking feature is "that it pulls itself up by its own bootstraps and becomes distinct from its environment through its own dynamics, in such a way that both things are inseparable."[5] The being and doing of an autopoietic organization are inseparable, which actually constitutes the core of their specific mode of organization. The authors nevertheless fail to indicate why they believe that the autopoietic system starts only at the level of biology. The process they describe as being autopoietic seems related to self-reference and its relation to the creation of higher levels. These processes are operating in the whole realm of reality and not just from the biological level onward. Acknowledging that fact is important, for it opens up a whole new domain where evolutionary processes can and should be studied.

It may be that some of the reasons behind a restrictive approach to evolution—namely, the assumption that evolution operates only in biology and onward—can be found in the history of evolution as a scientific perspective. Biology, after all, was the first discipline in which the basic elements of an evolutionary theory were expressed. Evolution is the model that we have accepted and have successfully used to describe the increasing complexity and adaptability of biological organisms in relation to their environment. Biology, therefore, seems to have a patent on the use of the notion of evolution.

The more or less exclusive identification of specific terminology with a specific discipline is not restricted to biology. John Deely makes a relevant heuristic remark about the fact that, for a long time, philosophy of science has been more or less identical to philosophy of physics. After all, as he points out, the revolution in our conception of the world as well as the technology that dramatically increased our control over the material order are "in large part results of the detailed development and extensive application of the mathematical schema definitive of physics in the modern sense of the word."[6]

It seems reasonable, then, to assume that the combination of the discipline-specific traditions of the theory of evolution, on the one hand, and the philosophy of science, on the other, causes, precisely because of the initial success in a specific discipline, a certain resistance against using "evolution" as a central onto-epistemic notion. It almost seems as if biology—maybe we should say "biologists"—wants to keep evolution to itself, while physics does not want to hear about it. Paul Davies, in *God and the New Physics*, makes an observation about the relation between physics and biology as it developed in light of the "new physics." "It is ironical," Davies remarks, "that physics, which has led the way for all other sciences, is now moving towards a more accommodating view of mind, while the life sciences, following the path of last century's physics, are trying to abolish mind altogether."[7] Davies' remark seems to suggest that biology might be stuck in a mechanistic, reductionist framework. The question arises whether such a perspective is consistent or even compatible with the notion of evolution, or whether this is indeed an indication that biology wants to maintain strict control over evolution by not allowing anything else to evolve out of biological organisms. Nevertheless, it seems to me that the recent developments in quantum physics, which I will further elaborate on in the next chapter, hint at a more general, more interdisciplinarity-oriented use of "evolution" as a central onto-epistemic notion, not only in physics, but on all levels of reality.

Why the restriction of evolution to biology? Consequently, why the restriction of genuine language to the cultural domain of the human species? Is there an additional condition or variable, other than those inherent to any evolutionary structure, that should be taken into account in order for a system to qualify as a language? According to Maturana and Varela, the so-called language of bees is not genuinely a language, because the linguistic domain of an organism, in their opinion, is restricted to the domain of all its *ontogenic,* or learned, communicative behavior. In the case of bee language, the basic behavioral coordination is *phylogenetic,* or innate, with only some minor variations or "dialects" that are ontogenetically determined. In other words, the stability of the "instinctive" communicative behavior of bees is dependent upon the genetic stability of the species and "not on the cultural stability of the social system in which they take place."[8] While Maturana and Varela identify the action of knowing as dealing with language, they restrict the domain of knowledge to actions that are socially and culturally determined—even though they assert that "there is no discontinuity between what is social and what is human and their biological roots."[9]

Maturana and Varela do not go so far as to claim that linguistic behavior pertains only to human beings. But they do claim that when an organism, operating in a linguistic environment, can describe itself and its linguistic behavior as part of the linguistic environment, we reach a new phenomenal domain, the "domain of language," which in turn leads to reflection and consciousness. The good news here is that Maturana and Varela explicitly introduce self-reference as being essential to language: "We are in language or, better, we 'language' only when through a reflexive action we make a linguistic distinction of a linguistic distinction."[10] But I fail to understand why language should be introduced as an operation on linguistic behavior, especially when linguistic behavior is defined in terms of, or in relation to, a cultural and social environment of autopoetic or "living" organisms.

I guess that Maturana and Varela are desperately trying to unconditionally guarantee the uniqueness of human beings. The authors are probably right to claim that language—our human language—is unique, because it is a linguistic reflection on a linguistic operation. The point to make, however, is not that our language is so unique, but rather that the underlying system, based on reflexivity, is as such not unique to a human environment. Our human language as well as our humanity as such are indeed unique, because they are based on reflexivity within a unique domain. But that domain itself—humanity—is as such the solution to problems, the paradoxes, caused by reflexivity on the preceding levels of complexity. In turn, those preceding levels are, with respect to their own "ancestors," as unique and as new as the human level is with respect to the environment out of which it has emerged.

Biological and cultural evolution cannot be understood independently from what precedes them. The question concerning evolution in general is basically the question concerning history or, more precisely, prehistory. Biological evolution, in particular, cannot be properly understood unless it is viewed as an extension of those historical roots.

In chapter 2, I indicated that Husserl makes basically a related mistake when he defines the horizon of the interdisciplinary project as historical. The history of knowledge, according to Husserl, is part of a larger historical project, embracing the totality of the universal historicity of humanity and the cultural world. Nevertheless, Husserl assumes that the questions related to specific parts, such as geometry, have a closed character and should not be investigated beyond their prescientific materials.

In order to establish an interdisciplinary project, it is necessary to investigate our historical roots beyond Husserl's prescientific material or Maturana and Varela's autopoetic organization. Such a history (or evolution, as I prefer to call it) is exactly what provides us with the anchors for our language—anchors linking our human languages to the languages of the world.

An irreducibly probabilistic and fundamentally evolutionary interpretation of the totality of reality is not, of course, the most intuitive nor the most complete one might wish to have. But, on the other hand, it is neither a trivial nor a completely arbitrary interpretation. It is this intrinsic nontrivial incompleteness, I believe, that makes probabilistic evolution in principle a plausible candidate to play the role of a central onto-epistemic notion.

Biologist and UNESCO director Julian Huxley described three main regions in which evolution is operative in different ways: the inorganic or cosmological; the organic or biological; and the human or psychoverbal. Besides differences related to their extent in space and time, the mechanisms of transformation operating within each of these regions, their results, and the levels of organization they attain, these regions also differ in their relation to each other. Each region, according to Huxley, is possible only on the basis of the previous region, "so that, although all three are in operation today, their origins succeeded each other in time. There was a critical point to be surmounted before the second could arise out of the first, or the third out of the second."[11]

Even though we might question the effectiveness and the completeness of the three specific levels introduced by Huxley—presumably it will at least be necessary to describe a more intricate network of sublevels—I believe that his approach adequately establishes a general structure of evolution as an interdisciplinary process, with paradoxes as the "critical points" to be surmounted before one level of complexity can evolve into the next. Even stronger: In such a structure, paradoxes appear less as obstacles making it difficult to reach the next level than as bottlenecks making it necessary to jump to a next level.

If evolution is established as an intrinsically interdisciplinary perspective, and I propose it should be, then it ought to be subject to the conditions for interdisciplinarity outlined in the previous chapters. This implies, among other things, that evolution has to be subject to some form of evolutionary change that accounts for the irreducible character of individual disciplines. Unless we want to claim that "biology = epistemology," there is no way that scientific evolution is going to be the literal extension of biological evolution that Hahlweg and Hooker claim it is.[12]

Literal is the operative word here. That evolution on the level of cognition is literally an extension of evolution on the level of biology—to which I subscribe—should not be necessarily construed as a "literal extension," subject to the critique of the primacy of literal verbal language that I presented in chapter 3. Hahlweg and Hooker assume the existence of a one-to-one relation between evolutionary mechanisms on the level of biological structures and evolutionary mechanisms on the level of scientific research. They establish a general framework to deal with biological, cognitive, and scientific evolution that is based on two dichotomies: the distinction between individuals and populations, on the one hand, and the distinction between informational and causal characterizations of physical systems and their processes, on the other.[13] The distinction between individuals and populations stresses that individuals develop while populations evolve: Selection operates on the variations in a population and not in individuals. The second dichotomy relates to the distinction between heredity, or the informational aspects of genes and the changes thereof, and mutation, which is caused by physical and chemical processes. Hahlweg and Hooker proceed to illustrate a structural isomorphism between biological and scientific evolution. They ask what could be the source of this relationship. In an answer to this question, their respective views diverge. Hahlberg sees a similar cybernetic system underlying both evolutionary processes. Hooker defends the stronger view that biological and scientific evolution are identical.

I have already argued that this strong view is not acceptable, as it defies one of the crucial conditions for interdisciplinarity. Disciplines cannot be reduced to one another. Hahlberg's view appears to be somewhat more sophisticated in claiming that biological and scientific evolution share a common regulatory system. This, however, leaves us with the question of how biological and scientific evolution are different. Hahlweg does not address that question. Neither, for that matter, does he explicitly claim such a difference.

In *The Hare and the Tortoise,* David P. Barash discusses the conflict between slow-moving biology and fast-moving culture. He makes a point that is similar to the one presented by Hahlweg and Hooker, but he explicitly acknowledges the important changes that occur when the evolutionary processes are transferred from the biological to the cultural level. Human culture—like an errant child, or Frankenstein's monster—"developed a momentum of its own and proceeded quite independently of the natural process that originally spawned it."[14]

Evolution on the biological level does not completely determine the use of the newly created tools on the cultural level. Barash, however, does not elaborate on the implications of his remark, which I find to be the most exciting part of his analysis of the relation between biology and culture. The implications are hidden behind his almost casual remark that culture is a descendant of biology: that the relation between biology and culture is itself evolutionary in nature and that evolution itself, therefore, is subject to an evolutionary process.

Two possible scenarios can be presented to explain how evolution can be subject to an evolutionary process. The first scenario implies two fundamentally different types of evolution: one form of evolution operating at the level of biology and any other level on which we may want to use an evolutionary terminology, and another type of evolution that could be most adequately described as "metaevolution"—an overall evolutionary process that is independent from, though maybe structurally related to, the level-specific forms of evolution.

The second scenario, however, is much more tempting, as it is simpler yet more powerful. Evolution is reflexive! This reflexivity cannot but entail paradoxes, which in turn account for the differentiation of the totality of reality in layers of increasing complexity.

This fundamental insight opens up a whole new domain where evolution can be studied. The whole hierarchy of languages, from quantum physics all the way up to human culture, is evolutionary in nature. In that sense, evolution of evolution presents itself as the grand narrative of interdisciplinary research. An evolving evolution can lead us to an understanding that is at the same time general and specific, all-embracing and nontrivial. It can account for distinctions and relations, for the apparent contradictions in history. An evolving evolution is extremely flexible, yet relatively simple and consistent in its processes.

Evolution of evolution does away with the requirement that exactly the same processes should be governing the creation of variations and their selection on all the levels of reality. Although I most certainly want to argue that culture, like biological systems, is literally subjected to evolutionary processes, the relation between evolution on the level of biology and evolution on the level of culture cannot be considered to be literal. It is in principle impossible to map biological evolutionary processes onto cultural evolution: If such a one-to-one mapping were possible at all, the biological and the cultural would coincide completely. Biology and culture would collapse to a single layer of complexity.

It is at this point that the role of figurative language becomes crucial: The relation between the evolutionary processes on different levels of reality, including the feedback whereby, for example, cultural events will affect the biological level, is figurative in nature and can, I believe, be dealt with and accounted for only in figurative language. If the evolution of evolution is indeed a form of figurative language operating in the world—I shall attempt to substantiate this hypothesis—then only figurative language can adequately make those processes accessible to us, in exactly the same way as Paul Klee's *Schöpferische Konfession* provides us with a better understanding of the world of figurative visual thinking.

Performing Language

The evolutionary approach outlined so far in this chapter radically breaks with the traditional views of language as a primarily human tool for communication. These theories imply that language is more or less independent of what is communicated—knowledge—and what that knowledge refers to. Viewing the evolutionary process as a basic, if not the most basic, performance, I propose a less arbitrary relation between our language and the knowledge it expresses or contains, on the one hand, and the world it refers to, on the other hand. More precisely, I suggest that the extent to which we are able to perform in the world constitutes the extent of our knowledge about the world, and therefore constitutes our world.

This is not just a pragmatist, utilitarian approach to knowledge and the world, at least not in the traditional sense of that terminology. It is, however, an approach implying that, for instance, the extent to which our stomach reacts to what we eat is a part of our knowledge of the world, and that it constitutes the world from our stomach's point of view. We do not *have* knowledge that tells our stomach, our intestines, our brain, and all the other organs involved in the process of digesting food what they should do when we eat. The very complex interactions among these organs, as well as the individual performances of each of them, *constitute* that part of our knowledge of the world. When I cut my finger with a knife, this cut, as a physical reaction of my skin, is part of my knowledge of what is going on in my environment. Although my skin has no concept of a knife as a functional object and has no idea about the knife's relation to a fork, it literally knows what a knife is, to the extent that some of the knife's properties are available to it and that it reacts to the knife. But of course, I know much more about the knife and the fork than my skin does—I can even tell an entertaining story about how some medieval French princess got married to an Italian and how the priests cried out against her, because her dowry contained a sure sign of decadence—a fork. The point is that the totality of my knowledge consists of the interaction among all those levels operating simultaneously.

Another example. To the extent that a rock is able to maintain itself in a stable position, or to the extent that it falls when it is dropped from a certain height or when it is hit by another rock, the rock has knowledge of the world. The falling of the rock when it is dropped constitutes the rock's knowledge of its environment, of the world. The knowledge is there *in the act of falling*, in the interaction with an environment. In other words, *performance is knowledge* and *knowledge is performance. Knowledge is performance of language.*

I am well aware that this is a very strong claim. At the same time, however, it is a minimal claim, consistent with the conditions for interdisciplinarity introduced in chapter 2. It does not account for what makes us different from the rock—regardless of whether we want to express this difference in terms of a subject-object distinction, intentionality, or having a soul. But this is again to argue that we have more in common with a rock than is apparent to us. Not only do we always exist on a physical level that we share with a rock—rocks and other physical bodies are as such not any wiser than we are as physical bodies—but our distinct features are not "given" to us from the very beginning: We develop them gradually. We do not have sensory experience of the world from the very moment of our conception onward. We do not make a subject-object distinction immediately after we are born.

In a strange way, however, it can be argued that we do not make a subject-object distinction immediately after birth because at that point we are still too different from our environment. We need to become more like our environment before it even makes sense to start pointing out differences. What we have in common with our environment serves as the basis for our unique, human features. In that sense, we need to be "like our environment" before we can become human, just as a rock, as any physical object, must to some extent take part in what goes on at the indeterminate quantum world before it can establish itself in the physical and chemical world as a relatively stable entity with highly specific properties.

Epigenetic Redundancy

In this section, I will present some of the evidence available to substantiate the hypothesis that we must be like our environment in order for distinctions to be meaningful. This hypothesis is important, for it provides a firm foundation for the need for interdisciplinarity in order to fully understand the specifics of each of the individual disciplines.

From the beginning of this century onward, an increasing amount of evidence has been found to support the hypothesis that nerve tissue degenerates, as if certain nerve cells die off. The phenomenon has been found to appear systematically during neural development. Counting the neurons along a motor nucleus of a chicken, V. Hamburger found a drop from twenty thousand neurons in an embryo five and a half days old to twelve thousand neurons in an adult chicken: a decrease of 40 percent. The process, however, is not uniform: After an initial, spectacular decrease of neurons between the sixth and ninth days, the cell death slows down to a much lower rate.

Similar processes are found in the peripheral, as well as in the central, nervous system. Changeux concludes from this evidence that the initial nervous system is redundant as well as diffuse. Later, however, the system changes. It becomes more simple and precise. The initial redundancy was only temporary, because the order in the nervous system is gradually increased by the elimination of nerve terminals.[15]

In *The Biology of Mind,* Changeux accounts for this process by his theory of epigenesis by selective stabilization of synapses. The basic components of that theory are the following. First of all, genetic determinism and inheritance govern the basic anatomical and functional organization of the nervous system. Secondly, adult isogenic individuals show phenotypic variations that are the result of the precise history of the neural development. The degree of these variations increases from invertebrates to vertebrates, proportional also to the increased complexity of the brain. Furthermore, the theory also claims that the initial growth of the neural network makes it redundant but also maximally diverse in its connections. This redundancy, however, is temporary, and the number of neurons and active synapses regresses. Finally, the theory of epigenesis by selective stabilization of synapses also suggests that, at the onset of the growth of the neural system, impulses are spontaneous. Later on, these spontaneous impulses are replaced by external impulses.

Experience, or rather "a sequence of molecular events, triggered by external stimuli," must mold the finer structure of the brain before the brain can start to analyze experience.[16] Under normal circumstances, the neurological aspect of our visual experience starts with an image projected on the retina—an array of some hundred million photoreceptors at the back of the eye that translate the image into impulses fed into the optic nerve, actually the axons of the approximately one million cells. The optic nerve in turn transports these images to the visual centers on both the contralateral and the ipselateral sides of the brain—particularly to the lateral geniculate bodies that relay the impulses to the visual cortex on the respective sides of the brain. We should not, however, conceive of this process as a single point on the retina stimulating a single brain cell. "Instead," as Briggs and Peat put it, "a ripple of activity spreads out across the cortex. As the signal passes up the optic nerve it becomes modified into concentric rings of activity or spreading ripples."[17]

Comparing the organization of visual pathways in two-month-old pigeons that underwent unilateral retinal removal either on the

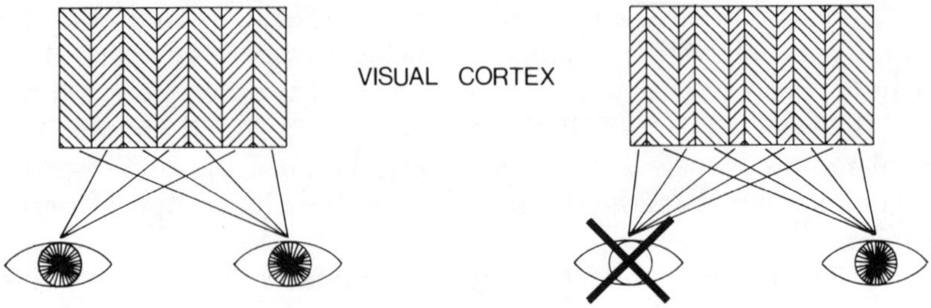

FIGURE 13.
Epigenetic redundancy. Resulting from failure of maturation, early-retinal-ablated pigeons show an important reduction of the volume of the contralateral visual areas. A similar conclusion is reached based on experiments with cats and monkeys: Development favors the functionally active visual pathway.

day of hatching (early-retinal-ablated [ERA] pigeons) or on the ninth day after hatching (late-retinal-ablated [LRA] pigeons) Bagnoli found that ERA pigeons showed a reduction of the size of the visual areas contralateral to the eye in which the retina had been removed.[18] LRA pigeons, pigeons whose retina had been removed after maturation of the visual system, did not show such a modification; the effect of the disrupted balance of inputs from the two eyes was restricted to chronic degenerative changes.

The ERA pigeons, however, showed a reduction of 30 percent of the volume of the contralateral visual areas. (See figure 13.) The optic nerve and some other components of the visual system could hardly be observed. These effects, rather than being purely degenerative, as in the case of LRA pigeons, resulted also from failure of maturation.

In their discussion of the experiment, the authors suggest that the failure of maturation does not affect all areas equally or immediately, but rather that some areas develop to a certain extent and then seem to wait for stimuli before they differentiate any further. In other words, the initial disruption at the level of the retina triggers a halted development of the next elements in the visual system, which in turn triggers a halted development of the consequent elements.

But the research also suggests the possibility of a *competitive interaction* between the ipselateral and the contralateral projection of external stimuli. ERA pigeons showed an abnormally increased and reorganized ipselateral pattern of fibers, while these ipselateral connections usually disappear and are not carried over into adulthood. Bagnoli suggests that this competition, triggered by visual stimuli, may be a basic mechanism for the maturation of the neural connections that process the visual impulses.[19]

Animals, including humans beings, that have their eyes at the front of the face have two visual fields that overlap. In the visual cortex, this overlapping is reflected in columns of cells that alternatingly respond to the impulses of each of the eyes. In the case of normal development, these columns are of approximately equal width. If one of the eyes is deprived of light in the critical period after birth, however, the columns corresponding to the useless eye tend to become narrower, while the columns corresponding to the normal eye become larger: The development favors the functionally active visual pathway. Mutatis mutandis, this result—based on experiments with cats and monkeys—reflects the findings of Bagnoli with pigeons.[20]

As an explanation of the reason for epigenesis, Changeux points out that it is more efficient to code a redundant neural system into the genetic structure and later change this structure in interaction with the world than to code every single neuronal connection.[21] Furthermore, epigenesis allows for a more flexible neural system. From birth through puberty, the redundancy is reduced in successive waves of selective stabilization.

Creating Redundancy

The evidence presented in the previous section indicates that our cognitive system is not the captive of a single moment, that it not only relates to the world as we individually know it, but also relates to the changes in the world, in our environment. Even in the very rough form in which the evidence is presented here, it strongly supports the idea of a fundamental structural relation between our perception and the language in which it is expressed, on the one hand, and the perceived world on the other hand.

I propose that in the process the redundancy of the neural network is shifted toward, or replaced by, an increased redundancy of the world. As the redundancy of the neural network decreases, as the neural network becomes more ordered, it also becomes less dependent upon actual perception of the world. To the extent that it has incorporated its environment into its very organization, the neural network no longer needs the accessibility relation with the world. The cognitive system can get by with "less world."

At the point where the neural network—or, in general, an epistemic system—has become sufficiently "like" the world, it can start pointing out the distinction between itself and the world in terms of, for example, a subject-object distinction.

What appears is an image that is no longer strictly dealing with neuroepistemic matters. What appears is an image that applies to the relations among levels of complexity in general.

The question concerning levels of complexity is obviously closely related to the question concerning complexity and/or simplicity, and therefore also to the claims of unified science that I have discussed earlier. Neither science nor any other type of knowledge is just the accumulation of facts and data. Knowledge proceeds successfully because of our ability to handle patterns, structures, and regularities. This success, however, could not be obtained without the existence of some fundamental relation between the structures discovered by science and the structure of the world.

The questions raised by that undoubtedly sound assumption—sound from a realist point of view, that is—concern what is usually referred to as "anthropic cosmology." Is the simplicity of the world an inevitable feature of the universe, or is there a plan that made the universe fit for our ability to comprehend it?

It is obvious that not all phenomena can be equally easily accounted for. It is harder to explain biological processes—life—than physical processes, although, in terms of quantity, our environment is much more physical than biological. Biology is harder to understand, because, as I have implicitly argued before, the biological level is more complex than physical reality. However, that still leaves us with the question of what complexity is. What does it mean to say that a process is complex? Can we even use the term in a meaningful way with only one argument? Or can we only *say* that one process is more complex than another—which would make complexity an epistemic rather than an ontic category. Is the onto-epistemic dilemma that we are confronted with related to a similar problem concerning probability, namely, to the question whether probability is the result of the limits of our cognitive abilities, as classical physics seems to suggest, or is it an objective property of the world, as quantum theory seems to impose?

A great number of approaches have been suggested. In dealing with simplicity—complexity's conceptual counterpart—Elliot Sober points at a wide range of widely diverging opinions on the subject: Some believe that simplicity is a matter of high probability, others contend that it is a matter of low probability, while still others argue that probability has nothing to do with it.[22]

The most obvious intuition about the complexity of a situation is to relate it to the number of variables involved. Francis Crick, for instance, makes the link between complexity of understanding and complexity of the world based on the increasing number of conditions imposed on more complex forms of organization. The conditions imposed on a living system form a small subset of all possible interactions in a very heterogeneous environment. Crick points out that during the earlier stages of the big bang "everything was so intimately mixed together that it was the broad outlines of the reactions which in large part dominated the process. It is thus easier to come to grips with them."[23]

If complexity is related to the number of variables involved in, or the number of conditions imposed on, a system, complexity could be a quality of both the world and our understanding of the world. This does not necessarily imply that ontically easy processes, involving only a few variables, would also be the easiest to understand. Because of our specific epistemic structure, which does not completely coincide with the structures it tries to comprehend, more epistemic variables could be involved in understanding some objectively simple process than in understanding some more complex process. The only valid conclusion this approach would lead us to accept would be that, *in general,* more complex processes will be harder to understand. From this follows that, again *in general,* a positive correlation will exist between the complexity of the language of the world at any given level and the language of understanding the world. That relation would hold for human beings, but also for any epistemic creature. On the other hand, this approach would also allow us to understand why higher levels sometimes seem less complex than lower levels, although I believe that it follows from the model that I have presented that new levels in principle need to be more complex than previous levels if they are to solve the paradoxes on the lower level.

Increasing complexity calls for increased redundancy. The redundancy of a language lies partly in its rules that introduce constraints on how an expression can develop, but that at the same time make it possible for a language—human language, but also any language in general—to express something at all. Without rules, there would be no difference in the probability of one message as opposed to another: All messages would become equally probable. As a matter of fact, we would no longer be able to speak about "messages" at all, since language would find itself in a state of maximum entropy and would therefore no longer be able to express or contain any information at all.

According to Elliot Sober, to render particular experience redundant is the principal purpose of knowledge.[24] This approach, however intuitively appealing and consistent with the epigenetic development of neural structures, imposes rather tight restrictions on what constitutes knowledge. Experience itself, to name just the most obvious restriction, could no longer be considered a form of knowledge. Only organisms that have sensory experience useful to corroborate or falsify knowledge could be considered cognitive organisms. Nevertheless, I believe that the idea of knowledge as being related to redundancy is interesting, at least if knowledge is introduced as the result of the redundancy of one language with relation to another. In doing so within the framework presented here, we immediately lift the restrictions on knowledge implied by Sober. Our cognitive system creates such a redundancy: It recreates the world.

The Interference Pattern of Evolution

Self-reference, in the context of the epigenetic development described in this chapter, acquires a special meaning. In referring to itself, the cognitive system, which has literally absorbed or assimilated some of the basic structures and relations of its environment, can and does actually refer to the world outside the system.

Self-reference is a special kind of performance that, as I have pointed out, directs the process of language toward its own output stored as objects in the world, stored in memory. Self-reference is a type of behavior that is characteristic for structures that can be described in terms of chaos theory and in terms of theories of dynamical systems.

Both the cognitive system and the world outside the system exist as separate but structurally related entities. However, in their interference, a pattern is created that reflects the addition of world and cognitive system, a pattern that reflects the probability of experience confirming the structure of the cognitive system as it developed. This interference pattern "solves" the basic onto-epistemic paradox on the neurological level: It allows us to be inside and outside our environment at the same time. It allows us to be both subject and object.

Recent research about the nature of memory has indicated that our memory consists of connections made by the brain. In that definition of memory, *brain* is not the operative term. A cockroach without a head can learn to avoid negative stimuli. Metals will remember events. Elaborating on that approach, we could present a molecule—a specific connection among atoms—as a form, or rather as an instance, of memory.

In both cases, the connections are made by language. Language creates memory. Here again we come across an exciting relation with evolutionary theory. Memory—as the persistence of a specific connection—is survival, survival is memory. By creating or establishing connections, language creates the possibility of survival. Life, for instance, is remembered by the molecules that carry it. As such, it takes on the form of a specific structure of a subset of all the possible molecules.

But survival, and therefore memory, is not an exclusive feature of the biochemical level. Memory is a specific instance of the general structure of language. Given a specific environment, atoms of carbon and atoms of oxygen will combine into a carbon dioxide molecule. Memory is environment-specific. Given a slightly higher or lower temperature of the universe, the contents of the chemical memory of our planet would be different, but not the chemical language itself.

In his article on memory in *The Oxford Companion to the Mind,* J. Z. Young refers to research showing that kittens lose their power to respond to horizontal lines if they are allowed to see only vertical lines. Memory thus seems to depend upon the specific selection within the original range of possible actions that represent useful responses to the environment.[25]

On the basis of the data, it becomes quite clear that memory is an expression of a link between a structure—a language—and its environment, which is itself a complex structure of languages. Memory allows for the feedback among languages, for in memory several languages can be present simultaneously. Self-reference itself is then obviously a form of feedback within a specific language, on a specific level.

The power of human language, of our human understanding, is related to the fact that we can emulate other languages (physics, mathematics, biology, etc.), including our own language or parts of it. *Our* mathematics is emulation of mathematics. *Our* physics is emulation of physics. Emulation, however, implies the involvement of a new level, and therefore, according to Gödel's theorem, the existence of true statements that cannot be derived from the previous levels. In other words, *our* physics literally adds true statements, true sentences to the physical world.

Karl Pribam explains memory as being analogous to a holographic image. In both cases, interference is the fundamental notion. In the case of a holographic image, the interference of two laser beams is recorded. However, in the case of memory, the exact nature of the process is not so obvious. Regardless of the discussion about the technical aspects of the model—which involves questions about whether memory is a matter of interference of electric currents, the flow of chemicals (neurotransmitters), and so on—the basic idea behind the model is that an interference pattern is a form of distributed information.

A holographic image, as a record of an interference pattern, allows the two-dimensional image to appear three-dimensionally, or even to *be* three-dimensional in a two-dimensional space. In a similar way, memory allows us to have access to all the sides of the house that we just walked around. Not using mirrors or some other tool, we are unable to see around a corner without moving around, without actually interfering with the world.

Memory is, I believe, essentially the record of that interference. From that perspective, the epigenetic development of neural pathways in the brain as the result of interaction with the environment can also be described as a form of memory, as a record of the interference between sensory stimuli and the innate structure of the brain.

Future Intelligence

Intuitively, and apparently consistent with the framework that I have outlined so far, it seems not unreasonable to think about human intelligence as a distinct level of complexity, generated by lower levels—in this case related to the chemical, physical, and other processes going on in the body and especially in the brain and the central nervous system. As we have as yet no good reason to assume that evolution has come to a standstill, the discussion about artificial intelligence (AI) comes natural to this work. In general, of course, the debate about AI is much wider in scope than my discussion of it here. It includes issues ranging from what it means to say that something is "artificial," to the cost of large, fast memories and connections between hardware and neural networks, all the way to what exactly AI researchers should be doing and whether computers should be given rights in the sense that humans have rights.[26] In this section, I will discuss some of the questions raised by AI that are related to the questions dealt with in this work. In particular, I will confront Searle's view on AI with the implications of the basic hypotheses I propose with regard to the creation of new levels of complexity.

Based on a specific assumption about the nature of the relation between mind and body, Searle concludes that artificial intelligence is impossible, thereby maintaining our preferred epistemological position as human beings. The general structure of his argument (A) is the following:

A1. Intelligence is a mental process.
A2. Mental processes are features of the brain.
A3. Computers have no brain.
A4. Therefore, computers cannot be intelligent.

The formal structure of the argument appears to be sound, and therefore if we accept each of the three premises A1, A2, and A3 in the form in which they are presented, we should also accept the conclusion A4. If, however, we do not want to accept the conclusion, we should take a closer look at each of the premises. It is tempting to change or transform structure (A) into (B):

B1. Intelligence is a high-level process.
B2. High-level processes are grounded in low-level processes (physical, chemical, etc.)
B3. A computer can function based on low-level processes.
B4. Therefore, a computer can in principle be intelligent.

The formal, logical structure of (A) is identical to that of (B). One could even say that to a large extent the premises of both proofs are closely related to each other. The major difference between (A) and (B) is the greater distance from an anthropocentric formulation that is maintained in the formulation of (B). In principle, (B) is not even level-specific and could easily be extended beyond the realm of human beings, making "intelligence" a much more general notion.

What this boils down to, then, is that according to Searle, life is a prerequisite for intelligence, even if we accept, as he most certainly does, that life itself is just a specific organization of lower-level elements. Based on what I have proposed thus far, I think Searle is basically right. But at the same time, this very argument seems to indicate that some new life—or artificial life, if that is how it should be called—is not in principle impossible, so that, even if life is a prerequisite for intelligence, artificial intelligence should not be in principle excluded—albeit, perhaps, based on artificial life. Evolution, as I argued earlier in this chapter, does not follow a single path from an absolute origin in the past to an absolute objective somewhere in the future. On the biological level, too, different species have evolved simultaneously and parallel to each other, leading to similar but nevertheless distinct features. If the notion of evolution is extended beyond the realm of biology, as I have proposed it should be, and if the notion of evolution is itself subject to evolutionary changes due to the reflexivity of the process, then there is no reason why we should not acknowledge at least the possibility of similar parallel developments within nonbiological systems.

Searle makes the point that computers can maybe *simulate* human behavior, but that they can never *duplicate* it. And simulation, as he specifies in *Minds, Brains, and Science,* is simply not good enough and often even irrelevant. Regardless of the computer's technology, "its operations have to be defined syntactically, whereas consciousness, thoughts, feelings, emotions, and all the rest of it involve more than a syntax. Those features, by definition, the computer is unable to *duplicate* however powerful may be its ability to *simulate*. The key distinction here is between duplication and simulation. And no simulation by itself ever constitutes duplication."[27]

We need to be careful with the terminology as Searle uses it. What Searle understands as duplication is obviously a perfect copy, not just on the level of our perception of computational output, but on all the levels involved. Such a position allows him to claim that computers—at least digital computers—are not intelligent. A computer is not a human brain, and if we could duplicate a human brain, the result would no longer be a computer, but rather a human brain. He makes it clear in his assertion that if we simply duplicate the human brain molecule-for-molecule, we would have a thinking machine, since it is presumable that if you can duplicate the cause, you can duplicate the effect.

If it is clear what Searle means by "duplicate," it is less clear what he understands by "simulate." He argues that it is nonsense to believe that the computer simulation of a storm will leave us all wet, or that a computer simulation of a fire will burn the house down.[28] The question Searle asks, then, is why anyone would believe that a simulation of mental processes entails mental processes.

Searle fails to make a similar remark about human understanding. To understand what a storm is or to say the word *storm* will not leave us all wet either. So why credit ourselves with intelligence and deny the computer that same qualification?

Searle's position seems fundamentally related to Chomsky's belief that human language, including its semantic aspects, is innate or, to quote Hilary Putnam, "hard-wired-in by Evolution the Tinker." According to Putnam, Chomsky suggested in a conversation that the difference between innate concepts and innate abilities is not really very important, at least not if the abilities are sufficiently structured.[29] That is precisely what leads Chomsky to a conclusion similar to Searle's: Language—in the sense of the rich human language—is something uniquely human. Bringing Chomsky and Searle together, thereby making the obvious connection between human language and human mind, seems to strengthen their respective views.

But the question I would like to raise here is the following: How unique is unique? Each individual human being is literally unique, no doubt about that. But that does not prevent us from communicating with each other. As a matter of fact, I have suggested that we are exactly sufficiently different from each other to make communication worthwhile. But not only are we exactly different from each other in the right amount, we are also exactly in the right amount more complex than our environment. Reformulating this in accordance with the anthropic principle, I have argued that we are different to a certain degree, both from each other and from our environment: That makes it possible to communicate, think, and understand, just as it makes it possible for our language to exist in the first place.

The "anthropic twist" is important, because it stresses how complexity—as it appears throughout the levels of reality—is related to narrowing down the options available on any specific level. It stresses how it is related to imposing limits on what can happen. If the universe had been somewhat colder or warmer, we would not have existed. We are the result of being at the right place at the right time, within very narrow limits. But this also means that everything that exists in our environment cannot be extremely different. It means that, as a matter of fact, the positive links may prove to be more important or more fundamental than the distinctions.

We may seem to be very different from the minerals and elements that surround us. In fact, there is a very important relation between the probability of these elements, which are the result of the scattering of material after a massive star explodes and becomes a supernova, and the probability of our existence as living beings. As a matter of fact, this relation is so important that from a more universal point of view it may be ridiculous to even make the distinction in terms other than "degree."

We are more like minerals, more like our physical and chemical environment, than we could possibly—even in terms of probability—be different from them. Because of that, and because of the fact that our knowledge exists on so many different levels, we can safely make the almost trivial claim that there is more knowledge in common between a learned professor and his or her ignorant student than knowledge that they do not share. But from all this it also follows that the conditions for the existence of digital computers and the conditions for the existence of human beings are closely related, and that computers and humans, therefore, share a substantial amount of knowledge about the world.

All this is not to say, of course, that the differences are not important and could be ignored. On the contrary, the point is that small differences can literally make a world of difference. The very fact that our own existence is subject to extremely narrow conditions—for example, on the order of 1 part in 10^{60} of the critical value of the expansion rate of the universe—should make it clear that even minor deviations can be fatal. The difference between life and death is, I believe, relatively minor, but it is certainly most dramatic in its effect. So even if we claim that the difference between the intelligence of a computer—whether it is digital or not, and even independent from the specific programs it can run—and the intelligence displayed by a human brain or a human being in general is really only a matter of degree, the result of these differences should not be underestimated.

Regardless of specific claims about the relation between computers and humans, note that these small differences will lead to ultimately different levels of complexity. But still, even if they would turn out to exist on fundamentally, irreducibly different levels of complexity, a common basis of existence of both computers and human brains cannot be denied. We should therefore in principle not exclude further convergence beyond the levels on which both the computer and the brain depend—a convergence, maybe, even beyond the levels that are already in existence today.

Chapter 6

Probabilities and Beyond

Wenn Philosophie das System der Vernunfterkenntnis durch Begriffe ist, so wird sie schon dadurch von einer Kritik der reinen Vernunft hinreichend unterschieden, als welche zwar eine philosophische Untersuchung der Möglichkeit einer dergleichen Erkenntnis enthält.
—*Immanuel Kant,* Kritik der Urteilskraft

The Quest for Consistency

In *The Origins of Knowledge and Imagination,* Jacob Bronowski attributes the "trouble" indicated by Gödel's theorem—that consistent systems contain true statements that cannot be proven by the system—to the axiomatization of the system. This leads him to the conclusion that "no formal system embraces all the questions that can be asked."[1] In other words, Bronowski sees Gödel's work as limited to an axiomatized system—which in his terms includes our human language—that is ultimately very different from the "real" world. According to the author, self-reference and paradoxicality are inevitable consequences of the cognitive tools we use. As I have argued in the previous chapters, these tools also include nonverbal and figurative language, even though they necessitate a somewhat different approach and though they are not explicitly included by Bronowski.

Bronowski argues that we will have to live *with* paradoxes and their implications. I slightly disagree with the tone of that conclusion.

I hope that in the previous chapters it has become clear that paradoxes are real throughout reality. To the extent that our cognitive tools are a part of the world, they too are prone to paradoxicality. Paradoxes cause fundamental trouble in the system in which they occur, but we—and all other things, for that matter—live and exist *by virtue of* these "troubles." That, of course, is a rather bold statement to make, and it asks for clarification and justification.

So far, I have outlined how paradoxes, Tarski's metalevels, and Gödel's incompleteness theorem can be brought together as elements of a generative system, leading to the creation of new levels of complexity each time the existing levels cannot integrate the contradictory features of a fundamental paradox caused by reflexivity. In this final chapter, I will attempt to use that generative system to sketch a theoretical foundation for interdisciplinarity, bringing together knowledge, evolution, and paradox in an ontology of language in general—including, of course, our own human language. I am afraid that the argument runs along more technical lines than what I have outlined thus far. In addition, it requires discussion of some technicalities proposed by other authors, but I hope that the reader who got this far will bear with me until the very last section of the book.

Doris Olin analyzes the argument that inconsistency is based on the fallibility of humans as epistemic creatures.[2] The so-called fallibility argument states that we cannot exclude inconsistencies, because our knowledge is imperfect.

In her analysis, Olin introduces the notion of epistemic probability, which expresses the degree of support or confirmation of a proposition.[3] The conjunction rule for probabilities is used when we try to evaluate the probability of combined events, each with its own probability. The rule states that the probability of the conjunction of two independent events (or beliefs) equals the product of the probabilities of each of the events. Since a probability will always be smaller than or equal to 1, the multiplication of several probabilities will yield even smaller results, even when each of the confirming events has a rather high probability. If the probability that it will rain today is .7 and the probability that my sister will visit next week is .5, then the probability of the combined event that it will rain today and that my sister will visit next week is a mere .35.

Adding more events to the series will lower the probability of a specific combined event even further. Very soon we will have to conclude that the world as we know it in its specificity is a highly improbable place to live in—which indeed it is. The flatness rate of the universe, to mention just one of many conditions needed to make the world right to accommodate life, has to be exact to 1 part in 10^{60}. What, then, we must ask, is the probability that all the other conditions will be fulfilled simultaneously as well?

Without going into detail, we can say that the probabilistic approach immediately raises the question whether epistemic probabilities can be quantified. We might even raise the question whether probabilities can be quantified at all. The probabilistic drop, for instance, conflicts with some endorsed epistemic rules: We are inclined to accept that an event A, which strongly supports proposition *P* as well as proposition *Q*, also provides strong support—and not weak, as the conjunction rule would have it—for the conjunction of *P* and *Q*.

This incongruity identifies a potential problem for an attempt to use paradox as a central notion on an epistemic as well as an onto-epistemic level. How can we hold on to a view of language as the operative system on both the ontic and the epistemic level, if the rule of conjunction of probabilities on the epistemic level is inconsistent with the rule of conjunction on the ontic level? If the probability that two events in the world occur in conjunction with each other is fundamentally different from the probability of the conjunction of the occurrences of our knowledge of those events, how can we ever know the world, then? How can we ever claim a fundamental relation between our language and the world? Providing adequate answers to these questions is essential to the potential merit and use of an onto-epistemic model.

What if the different rules of conjunction of probabilities are an important aspect of the discrepancy between the ontic and the epistemic? In other words, it might be worthwhile to investigate whether the changed behavior of probabilities is not an essential feature of the jump from one level of complexity to another. The shift from one rule governing probabilities to another then appears as a solution to an inconsistency—a paradox—on the lower level of complexity. Rather than being a troublesome side-effect of our epistemic position in the world, this might be what our unique human perspective is all about, both ontically and epistemically. Even though this approach is probably unable to explain the specific changes occurring in the jump from one level of complexity to another, it should—and it does—explain why the changes occur.

To make a more general claim about the relation between any two succeeding levels of complexity, and not just about human cognition in its relation to the world, it is necessary to illustrate that on every level of reality a tendency toward consistency can be found, ultimately leading to the introduction of a higher level of complexity whenever that so-precious consistency is lost. In that sense, the internal open-endedness of the world is the result of its drive toward closure, toward consistency and completeness. Furthermore, it will be necessary to illustrate that every next-higher level can indeed be described as an attempt to redefine the probabilities that determine or define the happening of events on the previous level.

The question then, of course, is whether we can even talk about inconsistency on the levels of physics, chemistry, and so on. If we regard physics, chemistry, biology, and culture as open language systems—and I believe we should—then it should follow that those languages cannot exclude inconsistency: Languages necessarily refer to themselves, and reflexivity unavoidably leads to paradoxes. In other words, the everything-is-language approach outlined in the previous chapters implies an intrinsic inconsistency of the world of languages. Showing that physics, chemistry, and all the other levels of complexity contain inconsistencies solved on higher levels is therefore also a strong indication that the everything-is-language approach to reality is a valid one.

On the microlevel, the wave-versus-particle definition of light—the wave-particle paradox—is probably as good an example of inconsistency as we can find at this point. The wave-particle paradox certainly does not appear to be a purely epistemic paradox: The inconsistency does not belong to our understanding of the physical reality, but rather appears to be an indelible part of that reality.

We have experimental evidence for both cases—that waves can behave like particles and that particles behave like waves. To set the stage for the further analysis of ontic paradoxes, let me briefly elaborate on that evidence. In two papers presented in September 1923 and in his doctoral dissertation of 1924, the French physicist Louis de Broglie was the first to suggest the existence of a fundamental relation between waves and particles, a relation that he characterized as being mathematically based on the momentum p of a particle—this is the product of its mass and its velocity—and the wavelength λ of a wave. His hypothesis about the relation between these two properties of seemingly very different concepts states that

$$p = h/\lambda \text{ or } \lambda = h/p,$$

where h is Planck's constant, the elementary quantum of action—the product of energy and time.

While a beam of particles that always behave like particles would cast a sharp "shadow" when passing an obstacle, de Broglie's hypothesis implies that particles can be diffracted as waves when they are superimposed: The wavelengths will interfere and reinforce each other or cancel each other out. As early as 1927, the diffraction of electrons that were reflected from crystals or directed through thin sheets of material was observed by C. J. Davisson and L. H. Germer in the United States and, independently, by G. P. Thomson in Scotland. These experiments confirmed the wavelike behavior of particles.

The problem, however, lies in the fact that this does not mean that particles are actually waves—"matter waves," as Schrödinger suggested. Individual particles can be counted, and their tracks can be registered. It is here that the paradox seems to appear: We accept—based on both the theory and the experiments—that particles are not waves, and that particles are waves. They are both at the same time, as is demonstrated by the famous double-slit experiment. (See figure 14.)

The experimental setting includes a shield with two small openings—hence "double slit"—and, at some distance, a second shield, which acts as a projection screen for the particles passing through the openings. When a light source is placed on the left side of the shield, and photons are fired through the slits, the photons will cast an interference pattern on the screen.

The obvious explanation would be, of course, that the photons in some way actually interfere with each other after passing

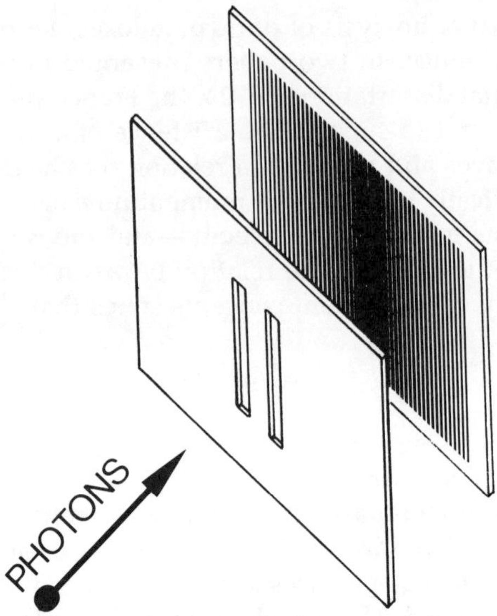

FIGURE 14.
Schematic setting of the double-slit experiment. As single photons are fired through the slits in the first shield, they cast an interference pattern on the screen behind it, as if the photons were waves passing through both slits simultaneously instead of particles passing through one slit or the other.

through the slits. However, the interference pattern appears even if the intensity of the light source is so low that we can assume that only one photon at a time will pass through either of the slits, so that, given the sequential order, no actual interference can take place! The only condition for the phenomenon to take place seems to be that both slits must be simultaneously open at all times, even when only one photon at a time passes through one of them. It is as if each individual photon could look around and have a basic understanding and knowledge of the environment in which it moves around.

Max Born was the first to suggest that the interference pattern should be interpreted or explained in terms of probability, or statistics. The probabilistic interpretation and the indeterminacy it implied were rejected by Schrödinger—who thought of the pattern as caused by "matter-waves"—and by Planck and Einstein. Nevertheless, the probabilistic interpretation of quantum physics seems to be the right one, and I believe that it is prototypical for the fundamental relation between distinct levels of complexity.

I speculate that a paradox—the double-slit experiment literally constitutes such a paradox on the quantum-physical level—creates an interference pattern that outlines the probabilities that will constitute or determine the next-higher level of complexity. The probabilities govern the behavior of the system of particles, but the system as such cannot be reduced to the level of the behavior of an individual particle.

A new level of complexity has been introduced. On that level, claims are made (true sentences, in casu the phenomenon of light, are uttered) that could not have been made before the paradox actually occured—before the individual particles passed through the double slit or before they were made to participate in the experiment.

This might also explain the problems related to the participating observer, who apparently is required for the wave-particle dilemma to appear. The traditional interpretation of the phenomenon is based on the assumption that a spectator or observer is present and that it is precisely the observation or the disturbance caused by the observation that causes the manifestation of the wave-particle dualism. How should we understand the position and the function of the observer? And what happens when no observer is present? The traditional solution to that problem states that the observer, although required, is as such not really relevant. However, if we understand the observer as a symbol for the partial reflexivity of the language of the specific level involved, the problem suddenly ceases to exist. As long as the system at that level is not reflexive, there is no observer, and the paradox will not occur. Once the system becomes reflexive, however, an observer is present, and the paradox will occur. What is needed is therefore not some external observer such as a scientist, but an internal observer observing itself. Such an observer is both subject and object, and it is precisely the self-reference implied by that situation that causes the paradox and therefore also the creation of a new level of complexity.

The new, true statements on that level do not regard individual elements involved in the paradox. In other words, the interference pattern does not give any information about the behavior of a single photon. The true statements, rather, pertain to the system consisting of a selection of elements on the level of the paradox. The new level of complexity leads, to some extent, a life of its own, even though it is formed by using a selection of material that already existed at previous levels.

Life, for instance, is not about the behavior of individual carbon molecules, notwithstanding the facts that life would not be what it is without these molecules and that we cannot tamper with those molecules without menacing the conditions for our own existence. And that is precisely the point to be made: While securing consistency or coherence with the evolutionary roots, the newly created level allows for novelty beyond what could possibly have been accomplished at the level of those roots—witness the paradoxes. This novelty can be expressed in terms of probability. This book, for instance, as an event in space-time, has an extremely low probability on the level of chemistry, a somewhat higher probability on the level of biology, and an even higher chance to occur once we reach the cultural level.

In *Particles and Paradoxes,* Peter Gibbins suggests that the paradoxes in our understanding of quantum physics are the result of the fact that physics is different from the physical world. Physics is a human product, a human way of representing the world. "Understanding the world" can therefore only mean understanding the way in which physics represents that world. And that, according to Gibbins, must mean understanding in what way a network of propositions represents the world, since that is what quantum physics is about: "a network of propositions, not of pictures, diagrams, iconic models or mental images."[4]

Although his approach implicitly takes the primacy of discursive verbal language for granted ("Understanding quantum mechanics must be a matter of understanding the logic of the words and the mathematics of quantum mechanics"),[5] Gibbins does prefer natural-deduction logics over axiomatic logics. Axiomatic logics, according to Gibbins, make "logic look like a mathematics theory rather than like something humans do."[6] Natural-deduction logics, on the other hand, in which a number of axioms are eliminated at the expense of introducing more rules of inference, are supposedly closer to real thinking processes. Since, as far as Gibbins is concerned, paradoxes are purely epistemic problems, it is only natural that he opts for a natural-deduction logic to deal with them. The solving of paradoxes, in other words, will require the introduction of a new natural deduction logic, NDQL (natural deduction system for quantum logic).

In order to arrive at NDQL, Gibbins looks at the lattice of propositions that constitute quantum mechanics. This lattice is as such not a logic, but at least it has a similar structure, which has to be made to look like a logic by matching elements from the lattice (its base set of propositions, the connective operations, etc.) to elements of a logic—the wffs (well-formed formulas), connectives, and so on. The result, which Gibbins claims to be sound and complete for the quantum-logical lattice, looks very much like a classical logic, except for some rules that have been thrown out and some restrictions that are imposed on others.

What can such a logic do? In what sense can it resolve the paradoxes? A strong interpretation (an "activist interpretation," as Gibbins calls it) proposes that the paradoxes of quantum mechanics can be resolved if, in our descriptions of quantum phenomena, we substitute a quantum logic for a classical logic. A weaker or quietist interpretation, on the other hand, is less ambitious and asserts only "that quantum mechanics, when it describes quantum phenomena in the elementary language, need not generate paradox, that the so-called paradoxes are not even formulable in quantum logic."[7]

The essential point of Gibbins's argument, as I understand it, is that the so-called paradoxes of quantum mechanics are caused by classical logic, which, in reference to quantum-physical phenomena, is a descriptive tool pertaining to a higher level. Paradoxes, in this approach, are indeed a purely epistemic issue. They are the result of the creation of a new level of complexity—our language, our talking about the world—rather than existing in reality and being resolved on a new level of complexity, as I suggest they are.

However, Gibbins himself attempts to dissolve the paradoxes by introducing a new level of complexity, talk of talk about the world: If only we understand that the paradoxes are created by our talking about the world, that understanding by itself should dissolve the paradoxes. "If the logic of quantum mechanics is nonstandard," Gibbins claims, "then the source of the paradoxes may just be our imposing classical logic on it. Move from talk about the world—one aspect of real physics—to talk of talk about the world—the philosophy of physics—and examine the logic of quantum-mechanical language and it may be that the paradoxes dissolve."[8] Gibbins's approach to paradoxes seems in some sense psychoanalytical in nature: Coming to terms with what caused our problems will supposedly solve the problems.

However, what if the remedy is the cause, or the cause is the remedy? What if a system that describes the paradoxes of quantum mechanics is itself a potential solution to the paradoxes? Gibbins does indicate that an activist perspective on quantum logic will fail, because quantum logic "does not *resolve*, but rather *embodies* all the strange features of quantum mechanics."[9] Our language, Gibbins seems to suggest, cannot solve the paradoxes. The only thing we can do is manipulate our language in such a way that the paradoxes no longer appear. We can add rules to our language that will assure us that we no longer formulate paradoxes. Gibbins concludes that a quietist interpretation of quantum logic, restricted to the microworld and thus not intended to replace classical logic, is our best option, even if it leaves us with the problem of the "gap" between quantum and classical logic, between micro- and macroworlds. "There is," Gibbins admits, "no way of pampering over this, except to say that the world is very complicated, that it has many levels, that life is larger than quantum logic (though smaller in some respects than classical logic). Which is no answer at all."[10]

It appears to me that a gap—a jump—between levels is actually a good strategy. It is the strategy used by the world itself when it creates new levels of complexity on which it can "forget" the paradoxes on the lower levels of complexity. In other words, the gap that Gibbins cannot bridge—because it is, as I see it, essential to the consistency of the world and should therefore in principle not be closed—is not purely epistemic, but onto-epistemic. The jumps and the related gaps are not just fantasies of overworked academics who are no longer able to think clearly enough to grasp what is really going on in the world. The jumps between objectlevel and metalevel are real indeed.

Bottlenecks of Complexity

Tarski intended his work on objectlanguage and metalanguage to apply to logical languages only. He introduced the distinction between objectlanguage and metalanguage to get a grip on paradox-prone language. Throughout this work, I have extended Tarski's approach beyond natural language, eventually applying it to the complex realm of reality. In particular, I have used his approach to describe the basic distinctions identified in our division of the world according to disciplinary boundaries.

Technically speaking, Tarski's approach is based on a series of distinct truth notions, each of which deals with the previous level. A concept True_i describes on level i which sentences are true on level $i - 1$, a concept $\text{True}_i + 1$ describes on level i + 1 which sentences are true on level i, and so on, ad infinitum.

Saul Kripke, however, argues that we run into a number of specific problems when we want to use Tarski's levels of language to deal with natural language. Apart from several technical problems related to high ordinals and transfinite numbers, we must at least acknowledge that such a construction is counterintuitive with respect to natural language.

Kripke argues that our language has only one word *true* and not a series $True_i \ldots True_k$. To solve that discrepancy between our language and the model, he holds on to Tarski's basic idea of levels and metalevels, but claims that we should use only one truth predicate—one that is "ever increasing with increasing levels."[11] To implement his solution, Kripke basically constructs an interpretation of a predicate, thereby using a pair of disjoined sets (S_1,S_2) as an interpretation of a predicate P(x) in a given domain D where S_1 is the extension of P(x) and S_2 is the antiextension of P(x). In other words, we can say that P(x) applies to every element of S_1 and that it does not apply to S_2. Outside the union of S_1 and S_2, P(x) is undefined. To give a simple example, in the universe D, predicate P—for instance, *is green*—would be true for all elements in subset S_1, which contains all green objects, and false in subset S_2, which contains all the objects that definitely are not green. The predicate remains undefined everywhere else in D, outside S_1 and S_2, where we find all the entities to which the predicate is not relevant—abstract concepts, for example. As we move up from one level to the next, both S_1 and S_2 increase for a truth predicate T (for Truth): More sentences become true, and more sentences become false. At the same time, all the previously established truth values are maintained: What is true on one level will remain true on all the subsequent levels.[12]

Kripke's approach starts with a level on which no truth predicate exists—this is a level with just empirical statements without an explicit truth value—and gradually extends the use of the truth predicate T(x), until, and this is important, the systems stops, because all the sentences of the original level have been exhausted, and nothing is left that can be decided by T(x). Adding a new level at that point no longer increases the amount of true or false sentences.

From what I have argued before, it should be clear that this intrinsically finite aspect of Kripke's proposal implies a dangerous closure, leading to a problematic system for which the world is not relevant—a system comparable to Hegel's and Derrida's. We must investigate, therefore, whether Gödel's incompleteness theorem also applies to Kripke's position, leaving the possibility that new paradoxes will be generated when a new level is introduced.

In Kripke's approach, a paradox does not belong to S_1, nor to S_2: A paradox is undecided. As such we should not worry too much about their effects. Paradoxes never obtain a truth value in the process of increasing levels. Kripke's approach (as well as Tarski's, for that matter) is simply an attempt to get paradoxes out of our epistemic system. That is all very well, if paradoxes are merely epistemic phenomena. However, if paradoxes are onto-epistemic—and I believe they are—we are at risk of separating ourselves from our evolutionary roots when we sidetrack paradoxes without acknowledging their crucial role as the driving force behind the evolutionary process.

One of the fundamental differences between a purely epistemic and an onto-epistemic approach is related to whether or not we can hope to ever "conquer" paradoxality. Kripke's model—exemplary for an epistemic approach—implies that, given enough time, it will in principle be possible to know exactly which propositions are true and which ones are false. At that point it will be simple to disregard all the others as irrelevant to our understanding of the world.

The evolutionary ontology outlined in the previous chapters, on the other hand, requires a much stronger position, a position that proposes that both sides of the paradox *should* be true and actually become true on the next higher level. An onto-epistemic perspective on paradoxes must therefore handle the new propositions related to the emerging levels of complexity. In that context, the set of events to be decided is no longer a given, but is itself a dynamical structure that cannot, as a matter of principle, be described exhaustively.

Figurative language—our verbal and nonverbal poetry on the level of our human language, as well as their counterparts on the nonhuman levels—fits the onto-epistemic approach rather well. A sentence or a proposition that may not be true discursively can be true when taken figuratively. In that sense, the sentence is both true and false. Any further use of the proposition—by which I mean a use on a higher level of complexity—will have to take that ambivalence into account. In doing so, the new level of complexity will at once become at least partially figurative, for it will contain a single reference to two (or more) related, but also distinct, propositions on the previous level. A purely discursive new level could in principle never maintain such an ambivalent reference. A purely discursive level would therefore be less, and not more, complex than the previous levels. It would have to choose a single interpretation rather than embracing some, or even all, of the possibilities simultaneously.

Whereas the results and advantages of level jumps are quite obvious, the process itself is not. Earlier in this chapter I suggested that a jump from one level to another might be understood as the reassignment of probabilities. A slightly modified version of Kripke's approach, extended to an onto-epistemic realm rather than restricted to the epistemic level for which it was originally intended, is consistent with that hypothesis.

Kripke starts his analysis of paradoxes with a number of examples in which empirical conditions of sentences involving the notion of truth—where, when, and by whom they were uttered, for example—lead to paradoxes. Such paradoxes, Kripke contends, cannot be avoided. No intrinsic criterion can be used to eliminate the sentences that could lead to paradoxes. In other words, it is in principle impossible to introduce initial conditions that can guarantee that a system able to assign truth values—a language—will never generate paradoxes.

Not only the empirical or contextual properties of sentences can lead to paradoxes. Gödel's work, while demonstrating the legitimacy of self-referentiality in general, in fact also demonstrates that the problem of paradoxicality exists in purely syntactic environments as well. Any language capable of self-reference is prone to paradoxicality.

While logicians will have a tendency to deal with the "cleaner" syntactic structures, Kripke reminds his readers that the examples involving empirical predicates are important because they point at the moral issues involved. The problem concerning paradoxes, in other words, is not just an abstract, purely academic issue without consequences for the "real" world. "An adequate theory," as Kripke puts it, "must allow our statements involving the notion of truth to be *risky:* they risk being paradoxical if the empirical facts are extremely (and unexpectedly) unfavorable. There can be no syntactic or semantic 'sieve' that will winnow out the 'bad' cases while preserving the 'good' ones."[13]

What I propose now, is that Kripke's "extremely (and unexpectedly) unfavorable" events can be interpreted as events with an extremely low probability, as events that for that very reason are unexpected.

To include figurative language in this approach as well, we must allow S_1 (the extension of a predicate) and S_2 (its antiextension) to overlap. Paradoxes can then be defined as existing not outside the union of S_1 and S_2—as Kripke proposes in order to get rid of the paradoxes—but rather in the intersection of S_1 and S_2. It seems reasonable to speculate that the overlapping of S_1 and S_2 creates an interference pattern that determines the outlines of a new set of probabilities that will govern the next higher level—probabilities, namely, that give more "truth space" to the "unexpected" events that caused the paradoxes on the previous level.

This of course relates to the idea that every new level of complexity literally adds to the world, just as our human language, which is itself such a new level, adds to our environment. In the process described here, more reality is created every time a level jump takes place to accommodate some low-probability event that threatens to get the system stuck in a bottleneck by causing a fundamental paradox. Every level jump, in that sense, is a "guess" about how the machine can be kept running smoothly, but, since the working of the machine is based on positive as well as negative feedback, small changes—the unexpected events—can lead to major trouble. Most of the time, a regular tune-up will be sufficient to deal with the problem; we usually do not get really upset by paradoxes. At some point, however, a dramatic revision of the engine might be the only alternative available—the information in the system is no longer self-healing, the problem must be analyzed and a new code protection must be installed.

All the great inventions in the history of evolution can be described as solutions to paradoxes on preceding levels of complexity. In the case of the wave-particle paradox, for example, wave and particle are given more truth-space in the realm of light—the next higher level. On this new and more complex level, matter can be wave and particle simultaneously, whereas on the quantum-physical level this is not possible. Light allows for the consistency of the truth values of both wave and particle. Consequently, light does not present us with a paradox, but rather it is itself the solution to a paradox.

From that same perspective, life appears as a radically new way to protect the information in the system against the disintegration of physical and chemical structures. Along those same lines of thought, our mind might be the most sophisticated device which the system has come up with so far, a device capable of experimenting with the long-term (paradoxical) effects of the solutions that it is going to implement. Literature, art, thought experiments, and all the other marvels of our minds are in that sense the laboratories in which we literally experiment with our future.

Paradoxes are, or can be, real. They are not just the result of our human language, of the language we use to talk about reality. Of course, paradoxes also exist within our language, but not exclusively so. Just as "our" paradoxes are the result of our language referring to itself, contradictions as we recognize them in the world are the result of the world talking about itself on each of the various levels of complexity.

When we say that *This sentence is not true* is a paradox, we mean that there is no possible world in which this sentence can be constructed as adequately referring to itself. But such a world can be constructed on a higher level of complexity. "Tout est pour le mieux dans le meilleur des mondes"—Voltaire's cynical response to Leibniz's answer to the question why God did not create a world with less pain, less suffering—is not the final word, at least not with respect to the problems raised by paradoxes.

Paradoxes are the bottleneck of the complexity that can be dealt with on the level of reality on which they occur. Paradoxes are a symptom of the limits of any level. These limits, as I have argued, are inherent conditions of any generative system. At the bottleneck of the quantum mechanical level, light behaves as both a wave and a particle. Going through the bottleneck solves that paradox by adding an arrow of time to reality: Light can be observed as a wave and as a particle, but not at the same time. In the statistical pattern created by the process of going through the bottleneck—almost literally in the case of the double-slit experiment—time gains a preferred direction, which appears to be absent in the interaction on the quantum level.

The great unification energy—with a value of at least a thousand million million GeV (one GeV is a giga electron volt, which equals one thousand million electron volts)—necessary to unify the electromagnetic forces that act on charged particles, the weak nuclear forces operating between matter particles of spin 1/2, and the strong nuclear forces holding together the quarks in protons and neutrons, as well as both protons and neutrons in an atom, might indicate just another bottleneck. But the picture is actually even more complex, because once through the bottleneck at the great unification energy, weak and electromagnetic forces remain undifferentiated until the next important event, which takes place when the energy drops, in the form of a cooling off of the universe, to a value about one hundred GeV.

What appears is a fragment of a fractal pattern of increasing detail, with each new differentiation or bifurcation characterized by a paradoxical situation, by a bottleneck that leads to greater complexity—more detail—of the overall image. The image of the bottle is interesting, because as opposed to the traditional image of the tree, it

FIGURE 15.
Bottlenecks of complexity.

stresses that the increasing number of differentiated things—the increasing number of bifurcating paths that appear—is related to increasingly restrictive conditions imposed on the earlier parts of the system. The bottleneck, as in figure 15, is an image of the conditions under which a system evolves and is similar to a fractal image.

Probabilistic Complexity

What has emerged thus far throughout this work is a picture of the world as a system of layers of increased complexity, whereby each layer originates as a form of partial self-reference of the previous layers. It must be assumed that new layers do not add to the amount of matter/energy in the universe, so that it may be more appropriate to speak of the increased texture, or the increased density, of the world.

Self-reference and paradoxes, as I have argued, are the driving forces behind this evolving complexity. A new level of complexity is created when the existing complexity does not suffice to handle the results of partial self-reference on each of the levels—an insufficiency that is precisely revealed by the paradoxes of self-reference.

The partial self-reference of each of the new levels implies that it is in principle impossible to reach a level on which complete self-reference can be obtained without at the same time causing the end, or death, of the system. If our language, for instance, were to become completely self-referential without remaining paradoxical, our language would instantaneously cease to be a language—an internally open system.

In chapter 3, I described two fundamental tendencies operating in the universe, and therefore also operating in language: first, a tendency toward increased disorder, implied by the second law of thermodynamics and the concept of entropy, and second, a tendency toward order, which I have described in terms of cybernetics and of which the existence of our own human language is a striking example.

It is crucial to understand that disorder should not be interpreted as a matter of simply more or less order. The linearity of our verbal language, especially of discursive verbal language, makes it hard for us not to think in terms of black and white, even if we do acknowledge the existence of a gray scale between both ends or extremes of a spectrum. We still think in terms of "more black, less white," or "less black, more white." In all fairness, I should grant that this is both a valid and a successful perspective on how parts of the world, be it on an ontic or on an epistemic level, are tied together. We can look at any given gray and describe it indeed in those terms.

However, a different, more figurative perspective is equally valid and should be recognized as such. This perspective is the one we discovered in Philippe's visual approach to some specific cogni-

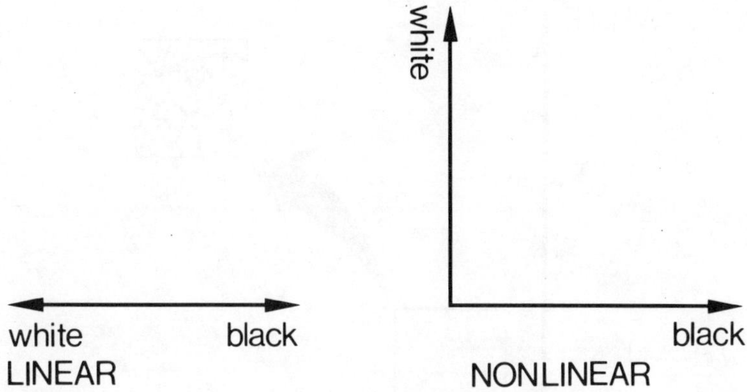

FIGURE 16.
A linear versus a multidimensional approach of dichotomy.

tive issues. It is the perspective that made him declare that the important thing is that everything happens simultaneously.

Within such an alternative, nonlinear framework, black and white appear no longer as extremes of a linear continuum, but rather as intersecting axes of a field of possible shades of gray. (See figure 16.) Both axes are at the same time independent from one another and intrinsically linked. Their interaction affects what goes on in the world and our perception thereof. Within such a field, black and white can simultaneously increase in terms of their presence in the field.

A traditional, mutually exclusive increase of either black or white can be seen as an increase of one, and a proportional decrease of the other, in terms of surface or volume (when mixing black and white paint, for example.) (See figure 17.)

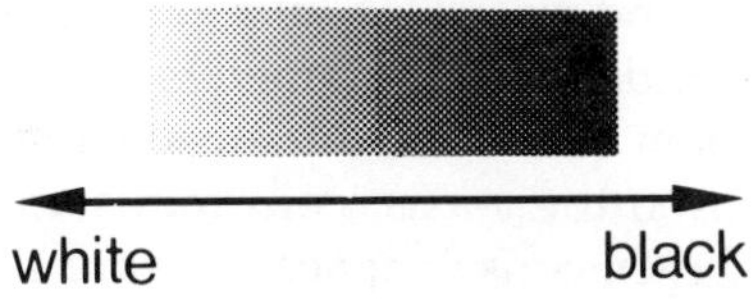

FIGURE 17.
The increase and decrease of black and white within a linear framework.

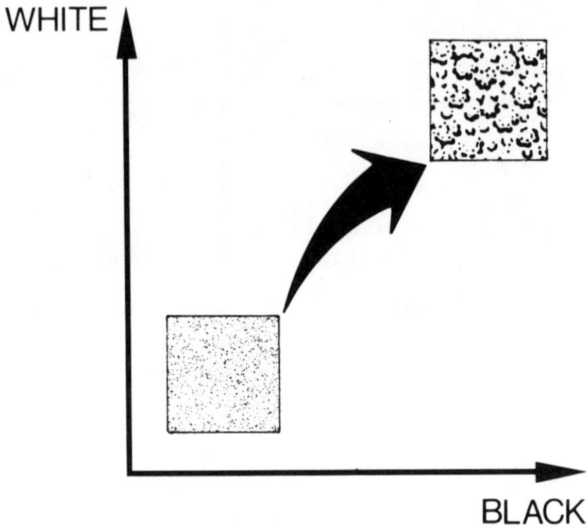

FIGURE 18.
The simultaneous increase of black and white can be thought of as an increased order, here visualized as increased texture.

A simultaneous increase of black and white, on the other hand, is more like an increase in texture. If we randomly distribute black inkblots on a piece of paper, we end up with an image that moves from white over grayish to black as more blots are added. When we organize blots into a lattice, we end up with an image that is simultaneously more white and more black. (See figure 18.)

Increased disorder is more than just less order, although there are some obvious connections between the two concepts. Order and disorder to some extent have to be independent from one another, because they can both increase at the same time, while one can also limit the other. Order and disorder—entropy and constraints—can be understood as two fundamental parameters operating in space-time. We can represent them in a three-dimensional model, in which entropy is represented on the y-axis, constraints appear on the x-axis, and the combined dimensions of space-time are shown on the z-axis. (See figure 19.)

Language exists at the crossroad of space-time, entropy, and constraints. An event that takes place is obviously not the only pos-

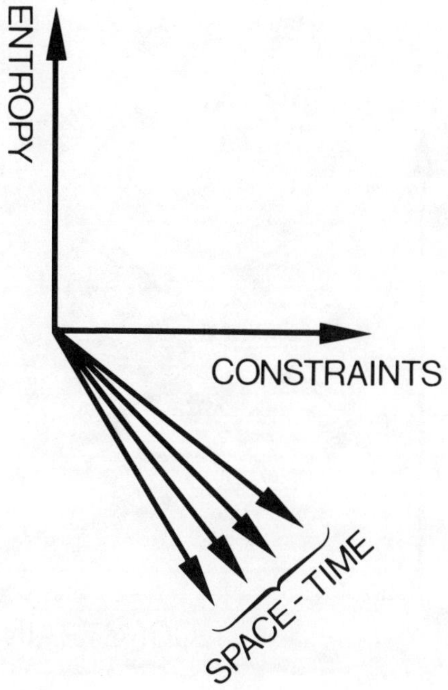

FIGURE 19.
Language as defined by space-time, entropy, and constraints. The relation between entropy and constraints can be thought of as similar to the relation between black and white in the previous figure. When entropy and constraints increase simultaneously, the order of the system increases.

sible event that can take place at that particular moment. When we utter a sentence, which is an event in our human language, that sentence has a certain probability greater than 0, otherwise we could not utter the sentence, and smaller than 1, for a probability equal to 1 would imply a completely deterministic world. Thus, a sentence is said—or, by extension, an event or an action takes place—within a distribution of possible sentences, as a choice between possible sentences. A sentence, an event, an action has a certain probability, and that is precisely what makes it meaningful.

My hypothesis is that probability can be described as the interaction between a range, or distribution, of entropic probabilities and a range of constraining probabilities. Together, they define a field of

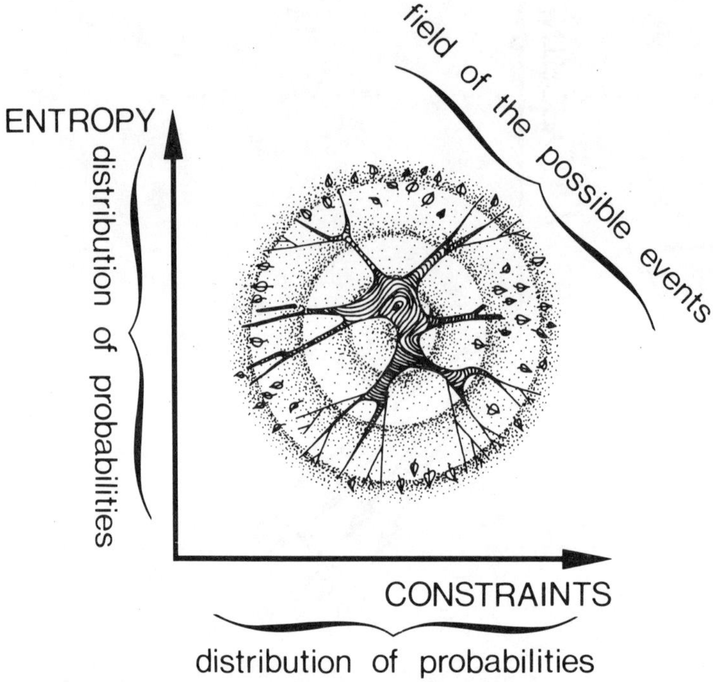

FIGURE 20.
The distribution and interaction of entropic probabilities and constraining probabilities define a field of possible events in space-time. The increased texture in figure 18 can be understood as an increased probability that a specific event will take place at a point in space-time and that it will not take place at another point.

possible events, actions, or sentences that depend upon the specific level of complexity. The interaction between them at a specific moment in space-time, but continued through space-time, creates an interference pattern that functions as a "strange attractor," organizing the events at that level of complexity. (See figure 20.)

Moving from one level to another literally means rearranging or reconfiguring the probabilities that defined or organized the previous level. A paradox is not as much a matter of black and white or true and false, as it is a matter of high and low probabilities. Levels of complexity are defined by the structure—the specific distribution—of the probabilities that are attributed to events. A level as such is organized as a function of that distribution of probabilities. Events, then, are informative as a function of their probability: An event with a low probability has more information value than one with a high probability.

The system, however, must pay a price for the information it obtains at a given level. Low-probability events, which can now be described as events taking place "outside" the strange attractor or as events "resisting" the strange attractor, can start forming a cluster of their own. When such a cluster becomes important enough, it may necessitate a modification of the original distribution of probabilities on the entropy axis and/or the axis of constraints, thereby slightly modifying the strange attractor to accommodate the newly formed cluster.

In case the cluster cannot be accommodated—when, in other words, a paradoxical situation arises—the original strange attractor can fall apart or bifurcate and create a more complex pattern of interference between entropy and constraints. A new level of complexity has been introduced. That will be the case when the existing strange attractor cannot be modified without simultaneously doing away with the solution to the paradoxes on the previous level. If that were to happen, the whole system would collapse to that previous level, and the whole paradox-solving procedure would have to be started all over again.

In principle, a new level of complexity cannot guarantee a solution to a paradox, it can only increase the probability that such a solution can be found. If not, evolution will have to backtrack one or more levels and investigate alternative paths forward.

If all goes well, however, a new level will be introduced when fundamental paradoxes occur. On this level distinct attractors will interfere with each other—hence the higher complexity. Together the attractors will interfere with the organization of the previous level(s), creating what we now recognize as the system or hierarchy of levels of reality. Interestingly enough, a cross-section of this process in space-time—a cross-section parallel with the *z*-axis—exactly leads to the bottleneck in figure 15.

In many or even most cases, the paradoxes created by a low-probability event will not be, or cause, a real problem; the event causing the paradox will simply not survive. As far as their evolutionary impact is concerned, the events causing the paradox will be put on a sidetrack, an evolutionary dead end. When we throw a stone into a lake, everything becomes normal again after a short disturbance of the surface of the water. The interference came as a total surprise to the lake, but it never really fundamentally disturbed the lake's peaceful and smooth existence.

In other cases, however, the unexpected interference will start a chain of positive feedback, leading to a dramatic reorganization, a fundamental redistribution of the original probabilities.

The emergence of life appears to be a low-probability event. Even though recent research has indicated that the odds in favor of a protein that makes life possible are higher than we previously thought (Dill and Lau, taking into account all the possible proteins with a shape that might become biologically active, come up with odds of 1 in 10 billion down from 1 in 10^{130}, life nevertheless appears to be an extremely rare event.[14] But life, as the result of the redistribution of probabilities—the evolution of probabilities—may become increasingly important in its interference with the universe.

The hypothesis that a major disaster, such as a huge meteorite hitting the earth, caused a fundamental change in the chemical structure of the environment illustrates the effects of such a low-probability event. What comes after it—the day after—cannot exist unless it takes those changes into account, unless it accepts those changes as conditions for existence.

Superstring theory suggests that we live in ten dimensions rather than in only those four that we experience; the other six are considered to be so small that they do not interfere with our one temporal and three spatial dimensions. Here too it might be useful to consider the other six as having a very low probability—in the sense, maybe, that it is extremely unlikely that an event takes place in those dimensions. Conversely, our four-dimensional structure could be an expression of the high probability of events taking place in them. They could also be the result of a low-probability event taking place in an environment in which probabilities were much more evenly distributed among the ten dimensions. Space-time itself appears, then, as a cluster that has added texture to an initially rather unexciting universe.

The Art of Probabilistic Evolution

A fundamental problem, as far as "traditional" scientists are concerned, may be the nature of the language in which interdisciplinary answers can be given. It cannot be a discursive language, because, as I have argued, such a language cannot operate simultaneously on both sides of the fence (or bottleneck, for that matter). Only a figurative—but cognitively meaningful and potentially true!—answer can be suggested.

We usually associate figurative language with aesthetic qualities of both the language itself and the objects it describes. Scientists, too, are often guided by the aesthetic qualities of the subject matter they deal with and the models they use to do so. Along a similar line of thought, Paul Davies also points out that physicists are often guided by the belief that the universe is intrinsically beautiful. "Time and again this artistic taste has proved a fruitful guiding principle and led directly to new discoveries, even when it at first sight appears to contradict the observational facts."[15]

I slightly disagree with the way Davies puts this; it is not *although* the artistic taste seems to lead to paradoxes that it can be a useful guiding principle, but precisely *because* it can deal with paradoxes without losing its referential value. The distinction between *although* and *because* is crucial to the explanatory power of the approach. The following makes that quite clear.

In his analysis of the problem related to the book of Genesis, Davies investigates the claim that "if the universe began, that means accepting it appeared suddenly out of nothing. This seems to imply that there was a first event. If so, what caused it? Is such a question even meaningful?"[16] The answer to that last question must be positive, I believe, at least if the framework that I present has any validity at all.

The emergence of space-time appears as the first event in time. As such, we can know that it took place, but we cannot know what caused it. The temporal dimension does not go back far enough, a hypothesis corroborated by the cosmological evidence that space-time was created in the big bang.

However, the framework proposed in this work does imply that time, as a radically new structure, was caused by a paradox in a world in which time did not exist, a world at the other side of time.

It is important to keep in mind that in that part of reality, *paradox, caused,* and *on the other side* cannot literally mean what they mean in our temporal world. They have no literal signified. They do refer, however, to that other world without being a mere shortcut for literal language: Through our figurative language we have access to the world on the other side of space and time. We can catch a glimpse of a world in which we instantaneously freeze, because the conditions under which we can move around are not yet fulfilled; space and time have no part in it. While we cannot investigate this land with our cognitive tools devised for a much more complex world (compare it to using literature to play Wheel of Fortune), we do know that the first event is itself subjected to the fundamental structure of probabilities. It cannot have had a probability of 0, for then it would not have taken place, nor can it have had a probability of 1, for in that case a completely deterministic world would have followed from it.

As a probabilistic event, the emergence of space-time is exactly like any of the other events that mark the fundamental level jumps throughout evolution. Evolution, thereby, is used as a central onto-epistemic notion, leading to an irreducibly probabilistic and fundamentally evolutionary model that is neither trivial nor completely arbitrary.

Is it reasonable to suggest that probabilities are what that world on the other side of space-time is about? We could argue that this world is the world of mathematics—not mathematics as the language of symbols that we can write on a piece of paper, but mathematics as the world that we describe when using those symbols. Mathematics, in that sense, is not a tool to describe objects and relations in our spatiotemporal reality. Mathematics rather contains the building blocks of everything that exists, and not just those of the world as we know it. That does not imply, of course, that our reality can be reduced to those building blocks. In the creation of the spatiotemporal world, some of those fundamental blocks were selected and combined to constitute a new level of complexity, just as in the creation of life only some chemical structures were singled out as constituents.

We know that the mathematical world is not a (Platonic) world of perfect forms, for it must contain at least one fundamental paradox that could not be resolved in it. Space-time is the solution to that paradox, and only time will tell whether or not evolution came up with the right strategy. For strategy is what this is all about: Evolution has put in place what is essentially a paradox-solving device. Are space and time not the essential factors of a world in which we can be distinct, even paradoxical, entities, only in a different place, at a different moment? Is not that what our sense of history—or sense of evolution, even—is all about?

At this point, I find it surprisingly easy to step in and out, back and forth, between our spatiotemporal world and the world "underneath," "beyond," "inside," or "before" our reality. What I find there is a world in which I feel as comfortable, as much as home, as in, for instance, Paul Klee's *Land of Better Knowledge*. That land is perhaps the world of beauty—a world of slightly broken symmetry. A world also with a tremendous desire for more complexity, a world with a need to experiment with novelty. A world, therefore, in which cause and effect are a partial reflection of each other, in which everything instantaneously feeds back into itself.

In setting off with a discussion of interdisciplinarity, this work embarked on a journey that has led us to a world of artistic realism. Such a journey, I believe, is exactly what interdisciplinarity is all about; it is to "look back to see how far we have come (opposite movement). We mentally dwell upon the way to that place and again to that place, which is now different (a bundle of lines)."[17] Interdisciplinarity, in that sense, is evolution looking back at its own history: It is the study of the evolution of evolution. When we will have completed the journey, evolution will be different once again—stronger and more daring in its quest for complexity.

Interdisciplinarity does not make the world a simpler place to inhabit. It establishes fundamental boundaries, a fundamental structure, outside of which we cannot go and outside of which we cannot exist. At the same time it requires us to be truly creative. That is the fundamental paradox of the language of humanity: that we will have to come up with something new that, while grounded in all the existing levels of reality, goes beyond what we are now. That is at least how we should orient ourselves, how we should behave in light of our limited and finite existence.

Our language, in all its forms—verbal and nonverbal, discursive and figurative—is the ideal tool for such an ambitious enterprise. Our language exists on all the other levels of reality and can simultaneously refer to those levels—our language is grounded in what evolution has accomplished thus far. It is in that sense that I suggested earlier that our language might be the interdisciplinary language par excellence.

I think that we have good reasons to assume that there are more epistemic levels of description than ontic levels. As I have pointed out in the previous chapters, the reflexivity of our language allows us to construct levels of complexity that go beyond any of the levels that we can identify in reality, including the level of our own culture. As a matter of fact, the fuzzy boundaries of disciplines discussed in the chapter on interdisciplinarity partially result from the asymmetry between ontic and epistemic levels.

As the evolution of the world progresses—as reality becomes increasingly differentiated in distinct levels of reality—the nature of the world's behavior with respect to paradoxes changes. At the onset of the system of languages, which by definition implies at least a distinction between two elements—1 and 0, in a binary system—a paradox means nothing less than a catastrophe. As the complexity of reality increases, the language system becomes increasingly resistant to paradoxes or the effects of paradoxes. Our language—verbal and other—in general, and our artistic language specifically, make it possible for us to cope with almost every single paradox without adding substantially new levels of complexity. As a matter of fact, much of what is going on in contemporary art could be interpreted as a quest for a new paradox that could lift reality to a higher level of complexity.

Art, it seems, is the laboratory where we can experiment with our future, where we can stretch our language into a world that does not yet exist, except, maybe, occasionally in the world of art itself. The extent to which we are able to perform or, more to the point here, experiment in the world (which I earlier specified as "interference with" the world) constitutes the extent of our knowledge about the world and therefore constitutes the world. In other words, I imply here that creative performance is evolutionary, and evolution is a creative performance. This performance must, however, be based on interdisciplinary knowledge. Art can be truly creative only if it goes hand in hand with interdisciplinarity, with the history of our own evolution. Interdisciplinarity is therefore not just an academic event without much use outside the buildings of universities and research institutes. Interdisciplinarity—reflexivity on a metalevel—appears as a condition for further evolution.

How is this possible? I suggest that the combined efforts of individual disciplines, interdisciplinarity, and artistic endeavors will change our environment to such an extent that we will become fundamentally different people. Art, in a sense, is the technology that we must use to link our past with our future. It will make us, I trust, more like true works of art ourselves.

NOTES

CHAPTER 1

1. Naubert-Riser 1978, 13.

2. Klee 1970, 1:76–77; my translation.

3. Biederman 1948, x.

CHAPTER 2

1. Heisenberg 1972.

2. Bulick 1982, 2.

3. Kant, *Logik,* A52–53; my translation.

4. Ibid., A54.

5. Kant, *Kritik der reinen Vernunft,* A644; my translation.

6. Doczi, in *The Power of Limits,* makes a distinction between "wisdom," which he describes as something that "synthesizes and integrates," as what envisions "relationship, wholeness, unity," and "knowledge," which is "taking apart," which "analyzes and differentiates" and "grasps only the specific and the diverse" (Doczi 1981, 127).

7. Sween 1991, 75–79.

8. Boorstin 1989, xvii.

9. Gardner 1987, 6.

10. Helmholtz, quoted in Einstein and Infeld 1952, 58.

11. Davis and Hersh 1981.

12. Hawking 1988, 174.

13. Heidegger 1982, 57.

14. The English translation (Derrida 1978) contains an especially illuminating preface by John Leavey, "Undecidables and Old Names."

15. It was not, however, Derrida's first essay on Husserl.

16. Novitz 1985, 103.

17. Derrida, quoted in Leavey's preface to Derrida 1978, 9.

18. Derrida 1978, 27.

19. Husserl 1978, 159.

20. Ibid., 166.

21. Derrida 1978, 28.

22. Husserl, quoted in Derrida 1978, 32.

23. Husserl 1978, 172.

24. Heisenberg 1949, preface.

25. Bulick 1982.

26. Cherniak 1986a, 5.

27. Ibid., 3.

28. Kant, *Kritik der Urteilskraft*, A346–47.

Chapter 3

1. Campbell 1982, 22–23.

2. Ibid., 23.

3. Kaplan 1984, 51.

4. Arthur 1990.

5. Miller and Johnson-Laird 1976, 702.

6. Miller 1986, 7.

7. Spivak 1976, xvii.

8. Renfrew 1989; Gamkrelidze and Ivanov 1990.

9. Lindekens 1976, 129; my translation.

10. Quine 1978, 162.

11. Ibid., 162; my italics.

12. Dowling and Harwood 1986, 2.

13. Ibid., 239.

14. Ibid., 2.

CHAPTER 4

1. Poundstone 1990, 17.

2. Tarski 1969, 66.

3. In Martin 1978. For a more complete historical overview concerning the liar's paradox, see Falletta 1983, 75ff.

4. Kainz 1988, 6.

5. Martin 1984b, 2–3.

6. Rohrlich 1987, 13.

7. Stone 1981.

8. Ibid., 449.

9. Ibid.

10. Hepburn [1958] 1968, 5.

11. Augustine, *De Trinitate*. Quoted in ibid., 16.

12. Hegel, *Phänomenologie des Geistes*, in Hegel 1969, vol. 3: 194–95.

Chapter 5

1. Lieberman 1984, vii.

2. Dowling and Harwood 1986, 4.

3. Hahlweg and Hooker 1989a, 3.

4. Maturana and Varela 1988, 26.

5. Ibid., 46–47.

6. Deely and Nogar 1973, vii.

7. Davies 1984, 8.

8. Maturana and Varela 1988, 208.

9. Ibid., 27.

10. Ibid., 210.

11. Huxley, *Evolution in Action*, quoted in Deely and Nogar 1973, 13.

12. Hahlweg and Hooker 1989a, 3.

13. Hahlweg and Hooker 1989b, 79.

14. Barash 1988, 4.

15. Changeux 1985, 217–18.

16. Aoki and Siekevitz 1988.

17. Briggs and Peat 1984, 258.

18. Bagnoli et.al. 1989.

19. Ibid., 526.

20. For a more detailed account of these experiments, see Aoki and Siekevitz 1988.

21. Changeux 1985, 248.

22. Sober 1975, vii.

23. Crick 1981, 29.

24. Sober 1975, 1.

25. Young 1987, 455.

26. A collection of essays such as Graubard's *The Artificial Intelligence Debate* (Graubard 1988) provides an excellent introduction to the issues at hand and the diverse solutions that have been suggested so far to deal with them.

27. Searle 1984, 37.

28. Ibid., 37–38.

29. Putnam 1988, 278.

Chapter 6

1. Bronowski 1978, 80.

2. Olin 1989.

3. Ibid., 100.

4. Gibbins 1987, 126.

5. Ibid., 126.

6. Ibid., 129.

7. Ibid., 142.

8. Ibid., 127.

9. Ibid., 144.

10. Ibid., 165.

11. Kripke [1975] 1984, 70 n. 23.

12. Ibid., 68.

13. Ibid., 55.

14. Nagorka, 1990.

15. Davies 1984, 220.

16. Ibid., 10.

17. Klee 1970, 1:76; my translation.

BIBLIOGRAPHY

American Psychiatric Association. 1987. *Diagnostic and statistical manual of mental disorders*. 3d ed., rev. Washington, D.C.: American Psychiatric Association.

Aoki, C., and P. Siekevitz. 1988. Plasticity in brain development. *Scientific American*, June 56–64.

Arthur, W. B. 1990. Positive feedbacks in the economy. *Scientific American*, February 92–99.

Bagnoli, P., G. Casini, G. Fontanesi, and L. Sebastiani. 1989. Reorganization of visual pathways following posthatching removal of one retina on pigeons. *The Journal of Comparative Neurology* 288:512–27.

Barash, D. P. 1988. *The hare and the tortoise: Culture, biology, and human nature*. New York: Penguin.

Barrow, J. D., and F. J. Tipler. 1986. *The anthropic cosmological principle*. New York: Oxford Univ. Press.

Biederman, C. 1948. *Art as the evolution of visual knowledge*. Red Wing, Minn.: Art History.

Boorstin, D. J. 1989. *Hidden history: Exploring our secret past*. New York: Vintage Books.

Bricker, P. 1987. Reducing possible worlds to language. *Philosophical Studies* 52:331–55.

Briggs, J., and F. D. Peat. 1984. *Looking glass universe: The emerging science of wholeness*. New York: Simon & Schuster.

Briggs, J., and F. D. Peat. 1989. *Turbulent mirror: An illustrated guide to chaos theory and the science of wholeness.* New York: Harper & Row.

Bronowski, J. 1971. *The identity of man.* Rev. ed. Garden City, N. Y.: Doubleday/Natural History Press.

Bronowski, J. 1978. *The origins of knowledge and imagination.* Foreword by S. E. Luria. New Haven: Yale Univ. Press.

Bulick, S. 1982. *Structure and subject interaction: Toward a sociobiology of knowledge in the social sciences.* New York: Marcel Dekker.

Bryson, N. 1983. *Word and image: French painting of the ancien régime.* Cambridge: Cambridge Univ. Press.

Campbell, J. 1982. *Grammatical man: Information, entropy, language, and life: The story of the modern revolution in human thought.* New York: Penguin.

Cargile, J. 1979. *Paradoxes: A study in form and predication.* Cambridge: Cambridge Univ. Press.

Changeux, J.-P. 1985. *The biology of mind.* Trans. Laurence Garey. Oxford: Oxford Univ. Press.

Cherniak, C. 1986a. Limits for knowledge. *Philosophical Studies* 49:1–18.

Cherniak, C. 1986b. *Minimal rationality.* Cambridge: MIT Press.

Chomski, N. 1972. *Language and mind.* Enl. ed. San Diego: Harcourt Brace Jovanovich.

Crick, F. 1981. *Life itself: Its origins and nature.* New York: Simon & Schuster.

Davies, P. 1984. *God and the new physics.* New York: Simon & Schuster.

Davis, P. D., and R. Hersh. 1981. *The mathematical experience.* Boston: Houghton Mifflin.

Deely, J. N. 1973. The impact of evolution on the scientific method. In *The problem of evolution.* See Deely and Nogar 1973.

Deely, J. N., and R. J. Nogar, eds. 1973. *The problem of evolution: A study of the philosophical repercussions of evolutionary science.* New York: Appleton-Century-Crofts.

Derrida, J. 1976. *Of grammatology.* Translated and preface by Gayatri Chakravorty Spivak. Baltimore: John Hopkins Univ. Press.

Derrida, J. 1978. *Edmund Husserl's The Origin of Geometry: An introduction*. Translated and preface by John P. Leavey, and edited by David B. Allison. Stony Brook, N. Y.: Nicolas Hays.

Doczi, G. 1981. *The power of limits: Proportional harmonies in nature, art, and architecture*. Boulder, Colo.: Shambhala.

Dowling, W. J., and D. L. Harwood. 1986. *Music cognition*. Orlando, Fla.: Academic Press.

Dreyfus, H. L. 1979. *What computers can't do: The limits of artificial intelligence*. Rev. ed. New York: Harper & Row.

Einstein, A., and L. Infeld. 1952. *The evolution of physics: The growth of ideas from early concepts to relativity and quanta*. New York: Simon & Schuster.

Erickson, S. A. 1970. *Language and being: An analytic philosophy*. New Haven: Yale Univ. Press.

Faletta, N. 1983. *The paradoxicon*. Garden City, N. Y.: Doubleday.

Fraser, J. T. . Out of Plato's cave: The natural history of time. *The Kenyon Review* :143–62.

Gadamar, H.-G. 1976. *Hegel's dialectic: Five hermeneutical studies*. Translated and introduction by P. Christopher Smith. New Haven: Yale Univ. Press.

Gamkrelidze, T. V., and V. V. Ivanov. 1990. The early history of Indo-European languages. *Scientific American*, March,110–16.

Gardner, H. 1987. *The mind's new science: A history of the cognitive revolution*. Enl. ed. New York: Basic Books.

Gibbins, P. 1987. *Particles and paradoxes: The limits of quantum logic*. Cambridge: Cambridge Univ. Press.

Gleick, J. 1987. *Chaos: Making a new science*. New York: Viking Penguin.

Gombrich, E. H. 1985. *Symbolic images: Studies in the art of the Renaissance II*. 3d ed. Chicago: Univ. of Chicago Press.

Graubard, S. R., ed. 1988. *The artificial intelligence debate: False starts, real foundations*. Cambridge: MIT Press.

Greenstein, G. 1988. *The symbiotic universe: Life and the cosmos in unity*. New York: Quill.

Gregory, R. L. 1987. *The Oxford companion to the mind.* Oxford: Oxford Univ. Press.

Gribbin, J., and M. Rees. 1989. *Cosmic coincidences: Dark matter, mankind, and anthropic cosmology.* New York: Bantam.

Griffin, D. R., ed. 1986. *Physics and the ultimate significance of time.* New York: State Univ. of New York Press.

Haack, S. 1974. *Deviant logic: Some philosophical issues.* Cambridge: Cambridge Univ. Press.

Hahlweg, K., and C. A. Hooker, eds. 1989a. *Issues in evolutionary epistemology.* New York: State Univ. of New York Press.

Hahlweg, K., and C. A. Hooker. 1989b. Evolutionary epistemology and philosophy of science. In *Issues in evolutionary epistemology.* See Hahlweg and Hooker 1989a.

Hawking, S. W. 1988. *A brief history of time: From the big bang to black holes.* Introduction by Carl Sagan. New York: Bantam.

Hayden, D. E., and E. P. Alworth, eds. 1970. *Classics in semantics.* Freeport, N. Y.: Books for Libraries.

Hegel, G. W. F. 1969. *Werke.* 20 vols. Frankfurt am Main: Suhrkamp.

Hegstrom, R. A., and D. K. Kondepudi. 1990. The handedness of the universe. *Scientific American,* January, 108–15.

Heidegger, M. 1982. *On the way to language.* Translated by P. D. Hertz and J. Stambaugh. New York: Harper & Row.

Heisenberg, W. 1949. *The physical principles of the quantum theory.* Translated by C. Eckart and F. C. Hoyt. New York: Dover.

Heisenberg, W. 1972. *Physics and beyond: Encounters and conversations.* Translated by A. J. Pomerans. New York: Harper & Row.

Hepburn, R. N. [1958] 1968. *Christianity and paradox: Critical studies in twentieth-century theology.* New York: Pegasus. Reprint.

Husserl, E. 1965a. *Phenomenology and the crisis of philosophy.* Translated, with notes and introduction, by Q. Lauer. New York: Harper & Row.

Husserl, E. 1965b. Philosophy as rigorous science. In *Phenomenology and the crisis of philosophy.* See Husserl 1965a.

Husserl, E. 1965c. Philosophy and the crisis of European man. In *Phenomenology and the crisis of philosophy.* See Husserl 1965a.

Husserl, E. 1978. The origin of geometry. Appendix in *Edmund Husserl's "Origin of Geometry."* See Derrida 1978.

Huxley, J. 1973. The evolutionary vision. In *The problem of evolution.* See Deely and Nogar 1973.

Kainz, H. P. 1988. *Paradox, dialectic, and system: A contemporary reconstruction of the Hegelian problematic.* London: Pennsylvania State Univ. Press.

Kant, I. 1982. *Werke.* 12 vols. Frankfurt am Main: Suhrkamp.

Kaplan, M. A. 1984. *Science, language, and the human condition.* New York: Paragon House.

Klee, P. 1970. *Form und Gestaltungslehre.* 2 vols. Herausgabe von Jürgen Spiller. Basel: Schwabe.

Kramer, E. E. 1982 *The nature and growth of modern mathematics.* Corr. ed. Princeton, N. J.: Princeton Univ. Press.

Kripke, S. [1975] 1984. Outline of a theory of truth. In *Recent essays on truth.* See Martin 1984a. Reprinted from *The Journal of Philosophy* 72:690–716.

Lamb, D. 1980. *Hegel—from foundation to system.* The Hague: Martinus Nijhof.

Lauer, Q. 1965. Introduction. In *Phenomenology and the crisis of philosophy.* See Husserl 1965a.

Leavy, J. P. 1978. Undecidables and old names. Preface to *Edmund Husserl's "Origin of Geometry."* See Derrida 1978.

Lieberman, P. 1984. *The biology and evolution of language.* Cambridge: Harvard Univ. Press.

Lindekens, R. 1976. *Essai de sémiotique visuelle.* Paris: Klincksieck.

Martin, R.L. 1978. *The paradox of the liar.* 2d ed. :Ridgeview.

Martin, R. L., ed. 1984a. *Recent essays on truth and the liar paradox.* New York: Oxford Univ. Press.

Martin, R. L. 1984b. Introduction to *Recent essays on truth.* See Martin 1984a.

Maturana, H. R., and F. J. Varela. 1988. *The tree of knowledge: The biological roots of human understanding.* Translated R. Paolucci, foreword by J. Z. Young. Boston: New Science Library–Shambhala.

Miller, A. I. 1986. *Imagery in scientific thought: Crating the twentieth-century physics*. Cambridge: MIT Press.

Miller, G. A., and P. N. Johnson-Laird. 1976. *Language and perception*. Cambridge: Harvard Univ. Press.

Nagorka, J. 1990. Signs of life: Earth's first organisms overcame tough odds. *The Dallas Morning News*, 19 March.

Naubert-Riser, C. 1978. *La création chez Paul Klee*. Paris: Klincksieck.

Novitz, D. 1985. Metaphor, Derrida, and Davidson. *Journal of Aesthetics and Art Criticism* 44(2): 101–14.

Olin, D. 1989. The fallibility argument for inconsistency. *Philosophical Studies* 56:95–102.

Popper, K. R. 1959. *The logic of scientific discovery*. Translated by K. R. Popper, J. Freed, and L. Freed. New York: Basic Books.

Popper, K. R. 1972. *Objective knowledge: An evolutionary approach*. Oxford: Clarendon.

Poundstone, W. 1990. *Labyrinths of reason: Paradox, puzzles, and the frailty of knowledge*. New York: Doubleday.

Priest, G. 1979. The logic of paradox. *The Journal of Philosophical Logic* 8:219–41.

Prigogine, I. 1986. Irreversibility and space-time structure. In *Physics and the ultimate significance of time*. See Griffin 1986.

Prigogine, I., and I. Stengers. 1984. *Order out of chaos: Man's new dialogue with nature*. Foreword by Alvin Toffler. New York: Bantam.

Putnam, H. 1988. Much ado about not very much. In *The artificial intelligence debate*. See Graubard 1988.

Quine, W. V. 1978. A postscript on metaphor. *Critical Inquiry* 5(1): 161–62.

Rabb, T. K. 1982. Toward the future. In *The new history*. See Rabb and Rotberg 1982.

Rabb, T. K., and R. I. Rotberg. 1970. Interdisciplinary history. *The Journal of Interdisciplinary History* 1:3–5.

Rabb, T. K., and R. I. Rotberg, eds. 1982. *The new history: The 1980s and beyond*. Princeton, N.J.: Princeton Univ. Press.

Reid, K. 1988. *Teaching the learning disabled: A cognitive developmental approach.* Boston: Allyn & Bacon.

Renfrew, C. 1989. The origins of Indo-European languages. *Scientific American,* October, 106–14.

Rey, G. 1986. What's really going on in Searle's "Chinese room." *Philosophical Studies* 50:169–85.

Rohrlich, F. 1987. *From paradox to reality: Our basic concepts of the physical world.* Cambridge: Cambridge Univ. Press.

Roskill, M., and D. Carrier. 1983. *Truth and falsehood in visual images.* Amherst: Univ. of Massachusetts Press.

Sainsbury, R. M. 1988. *Paradoxes.* Cambridge: Cambridge Univ. Press.

Schlesinger, G. N. 1985. *The intelligibility of nature.* Aberdeen, Aberdeen Univ. Press.

Schlick, M. 1974. *General theory of knowledge.* Translated by A. E. Blumberg, and introduction by A. E. Blumberg and H. Feigl. New York: Springer Verlag.

Searle, J. 1984. *Minds, brains, and science.* Cambridge: Harvard Univ. Press.

Sober, E. 1975. *Simplicity.* London: Oxford Univ. Press.

Spivak, G. C. 1976. Preface to *Of grammatology.* See Derrida 1976.

Stone, J. D. 1981. Simplism and the liar. *Journal of Philosophical Logic* 10:423–51.

Sween, G. 1991. Interdisciplinary disorientation: A student's perspective. *Philosophica* 48(2): 75–79.

Tarski, A. 1969. Truth and proof. *Scientific American,* June, 63–77.

Tarski, A. 1983a. The concept of truth in formalized languages. In *Logic, semantics, and meta-mathematics.* See Tarski 1983b.

Tarski, A. 1983b. *Logic, semantics, meta-mathematics: Papers from 1923 to 1938.* 2d ed. Translated by J. H. Woodger, edited and introduced by J. Corcoran. Indianapolis: Hackett.

Turner, V. 1986. *The anthropology of performance.* Preface by Richard Schechner. New York: PAJ.

Wallis, B. de. 1984. *Art after modernism: Rethinking representation.* New York and Boston: The New Museum of Contemporary Art.

Weyl, H. 1952. *Symmetry.* Princeton, N. J.: Princeton Univ. Press.

Young, J. Z. 1987. Memory. In *The Oxford companion to the mind.* See Gregory 1987.

INDEX